T0193223

PLAYING CHICKEN WITH GOD

For Everyone Who Married Someone
with a Hidden Addiction

SARAH ERSTWHILE

WESTBOW
PRESS®
A DIVISION OF THOMAS NELSON
& ZONDERVAN

WestBow Press books may be ordered through booksellers or by contacting:

WestBow Press
A Division of Thomas Nelson & Zondervan
1663 Liberty Drive
Bloomington, IN 47403
www.westbowpress.com
844-714-3454

ISBN: 978-1-6642-9592-6 (sc)
ISBN: 978-1-6642-9593-3 (hc)
ISBN: 978-1-6642-9591-9 (e)

Library of Congress Control Number: 2023905541

Print information available on the last page.

WestBow Press rev. date: 4/5/2023

CONTENTS

THE RETRIBUTION

THE
STUMBLING
BLOCKS

CHAPTER 1

Here I Am, Lord

Dan Schutte b. 1947

I, the Lord of sea and sky,
I have heard My people cry.
All who dwell in dark and sin
My hand will save.

I who made the stars of night,
I will make their darkness bright.
Who will bear My light to them?
Whom shall I send?

Here I am Lord, Is it I Lord?
I have heard You calling in the night.
I will go Lord, if You lead me.
I will hold Your people in my heart.

I, the Lord of snow and rain,
I have born my people's pain.
I have wept for love of them,
They turn away.

I will break their hearts of stone,
Give them hearts for love alone.
I will speak My word to them,
Whom shall I send?

Here I am Lord, Is it I Lord?
I have heard You calling in the night.
I will go Lord, if You lead me.
I will hold Your people in my heart.

I, the Lord of wind and flame,
I will tend the poor and lame.
I will set a feast for them,
My hand will save

Finest bread I will provide,
Till their hearts be satisfied.
I will give My life to them,
Whom shall I send?

Here I am Lord, Is it I Lord?
I have heard You calling in the night.
I will go Lord, if You lead me.
I will hold Your people in my heart.

Sometimes you do not know what you are in for when you turn your life over to God. I think most of us think it will be a glorious life full of worship and love. We see all the happy faces in church and think that those faces are still bright and glowing as they go through their week. But the truth is, when you hand your life over to God, answers to life's questions don't come any faster or any clearer.

As I sit here writing this book, I remember how my storybook walk with God began.

I remember taking my newborn daughter to church for the first time. Sitting in the pew, I recalled the terrible ordeal we had conceiving a child. We ended up going through three and a half years of diagnostic procedures for infertility, ending with in vitro fertilization. I recounted every struggle of the three-and-a-half-year ordeal in that pew looking down at my daughter as she slept. The countless shots with a one-and-a-half-inch-long needle for years—we literally took these shots with us everywhere we went since they had to be taken on a time schedule. Once I even had to shimmy my pants down a bit at a Bob Segar concert for a shot. I remembered the hot wires being placed in my fallopian tubes while I was awake, and the countless times we went to radiology so the doctors could check with dye procedures to see if my tubes were open. I will never forget the time the machine broke, and my husband had to literally lie across my chest to keep me from moving due to the pain.

The infertility treatments were quite a feat for my husband, a Catholic. It took a toll on his belief system. Being a convert, I was not bothered. But he really had a difficult time. I told him God was just using the medical procedures as stumbling blocks, not saying no. However, regardless of how I presented it, he was still in emotional pain. He couldn't sleep at night.

The pain seemed to come from not knowing what his parents would think. I remember the relief on my husband's face when he told his parents about our choice to get assistance conceiving. He found that they were thrilled. Their comment was "We choose life however it comes." Once we received that statement, the infertility struggle seemed a more bearable endeavor.

It was a struggle, but we did survive our infertility misery, and we worked together to make the in vitro process a success. When we saw the heartbeat of our daughter for the first time, happiness could not come close to describing our feelings. We were the married couple I had always dreamed of becoming.

When I looked up from my pew, I looked around the church. I could see all the smiling faces looking back at me. Many of these very onlookers were people who had helped us during the problem pregnancy. When it was diagnosed that I would have to spend the entire pregnancy in bed, my husband and I were a team with several of these people helping us. We had no family in the area, and I needed complete bed rest from the fourth week of the pregnancy to the day of delivery at seven months. During our problem pregnancy, the church came to our aid several times, with congregation members coming to stay with me while my husband was at work. There was a bond of faith that was beautiful. Even with the stress of the high-risk pregnancy, I knew God was present. There was no doubt in my mind that God had a plan. Even people we did not know heard of our problems and came to our aid.

As I sat in my pew with God all around me, I remembered how I felt knowing that God was in charge of my infertility treatments and my high-risk pregnancy. I remember the day they implanted the embryos. I said to God, "I have done everything I can do. It is now all in your hands." I remembered lying in bed for seven months, being rushed to the hospital to have labor stopped five times. The whole time during this messy, frantic pregnancy, I had a divine sense that if I did exactly what the doctors told me, our child would be fine. When our daughter was born two months early with no repercussions, I knew God was in control each step of the way. I was truly joyful and did not carry any resentment toward God for making us go through the infertility process.

I sat there and thought of my husband and how wonderfully he carried all our stress during that pregnancy. I was as concerned about his health and well-being as my husband was about mine and the baby's. We were truly a team, a devoted couple. As I sat there, I felt like the awfulness of the infertility years were behind us, and we were in love.

When the entrance hymn started, it was a beautiful song about God crying out for someone to help his people find him. This song touched me. Right then I said back to God, "Send me." You have given me all that I have ever wanted in this child that I am holding and this man that I love. "Send me. I will go, I will help teach them. Send me."

I did not know what I was in for. The journey was not to a faraway land. It was not glamorous or even fun. I was not even considered pretty, or nice, or wanted.

I didn't even know that I was "sent." It took me fifteen years to figure out I was "sent." And when I figured it out, I didn't like it.

I am not saying that if I had not asked God to use me for his glory, I would have had an easier life. But what I am saying is that God does have some mysterious ways to use people for his glory.

CHAPTER 2

I Wanted to Be
"That Kind of Woman"

You know that the testing of your faith develops perseverance. Perseverance must finish its work so that you may be mature and complete, not lacking anything. (Jas 1:3–4) [1]

Have you ever had the incredible good fortune to spend time in the company of a spiritually mature woman? Her presence, emanating from her gracious and fully open heart, is simultaneously soothing and inspiring. People long to be near her. She is warm, intuitive, and radiates the peace of a person comfortable in her own skin. Her comfort level with herself is disarming, allowing everyone around her to relax and be fully themselves. She is not constantly reaching, doing, or wielding her power. She does not need to. She is awesomely at rest in the embodiment of herself. She is complete in Christ. She lacks nothing. Her contentment is contagious, her peace palpable, and her influence divine. [2]
—Kristin Armstrong

Although I had just finished a monumental test of my faith, the polishing of my soul was not complete. I had survived the infertility years with my faith intact, but I was not the spiritually mature person that I thought I was. I truly thought I was spiritually wise. I wanted to be the woman described in the Kristin Armstrong passage: "wise and comfortable in my own skin." I think as we start out in life, we all want to be this woman, or at least know a woman like this in hopes that her goodness will rub off on us. But what we do not realize, or at least I didn't, is that God has to mold us first. We do not start out perfect, or even remotely close to this refined and glorious woman. We do tasks that we think are in God's name, but they are just tasks. We may think we are doing what God asks of us, but we rarely understand God's methods.

When I asked God to send me, he had a ton of work to do on me before I was useful to him. I was self-sufficient and very strong. I could tackle anything. I was an organizer and a doer. What I did not know was that I was relying on myself to find the way, rather than on God to show me the way. Unfortunately, I already thought I was a woman who was useful to God.

I was the church's "go-to girl." I got stuff done. What I did not realize was life is a journey with the hopes that we become "that kind of woman." Those women are not ready made. I believe every person can become spiritually mature, without worry, living a joyful experience with time. But becoming the kind of woman that everyone wants to be with, filled with wisdom and compassion, takes time and testing. People are on their own path, with their own timetable.

For a strong woman like myself, it takes more time and testing than for someone who already doubts their fortitude.

Why does it take more time? There is just more work to be done. The self-sufficient have learned to rely on themselves, not God, so there is much to undo. They have to be moved out of their comfort zone to a place where they need to ask for help. The weak are perfectly content to ask for help; they are grateful for what they receive, and they learn something new along the way. The strong and self-sufficient, on the other hand, just analyze the problem and maneuver around it. Although this is a plus for the short term, and tasks get completed in God's name, it can stunt spiritual growth in the long run. I find it ironic that the very gifts that God gave me, like being strong and capable, are characteristics that propelled me away from God. The stronger and more capable we are, the more we can become self-reliant. That is not to say that we do not have faith or that we do not pray. We just keep motoring along in life maneuvering through the obstacles that God throws at us. We do not learn from obstacles mainly because we do not view them as such. The gifts that God has bestowed upon us have allowed us to overcome stumbling blocks without much thought.

When we finally come up against something that we cannot handle, we pray to God and beg for understanding. However, we are also angry with God, wondering where he's been and how he let "this" happen. I remember being really angry for a very long time during my decades of testing. It took me a while to figure out that the stumbling blocks are a way that God changes our perspectives.

Stumbling blocks are the way that God "works," so if you think about it, they are really building blocks.

When we look at stumbling blocks as building blocks, it allows us to analyze our lives a little. We can think back in our lives to times that changed our thinking, times that helped us to grow into adulthood. Everyone has those moments they can remember that changed them forever. For me, infertility was one of those times. It tested me in a way I had never been tested before.

However, a few years after the infertility trials, my husband and I started to have other problems, much more serious than infertility. Our loving marriage had turned to a perverse one. Manipulation and lying were daily occurrences. All sorts of abuse set in.

When my marriage ended, I took a good long look at how I had changed through the years. I looked back through my marriage for things that I did right and things that I could have done differently. I remember first meeting the man I had dreamed of and how fun and brilliant he was. I kept telling myself that God would not let such a blessed marriage fail. Surely, I was not reading the signs of what God wanted me to do correctly.

I remembered how we started the foundation of our marriage by working together at volunteer events. During our first year of marriage, my husband and I were part of a group that started a new Catholic parish. We enjoyed the hands-on activities of clearing the lot for the church buildings and being asked to do things for the church community. We were a team of doers; my husband and I were equally busy.

But as each year of our marriage progressed in the beginning, my husband became increasingly agitated and very manipulative. Those infertility years were painful and expensive with no end in sight. I rationalized that anyone going through this would have behavior that was inconsistent with their normal personality. There were tearful tirades and drinking binges that made me think having children with this man was not meant to happen. The stress was immense. During the time we were going through treatments my husband's drinking habit increased, but there was a cause to our pain. We both were drowning our sorrows of infertility so to speak. Each of us blamed the other until it was determined to be a physical problem of mine. During the multiple attempts at conception, my husband drank profusely. However, we were dealing with so much grief that it was easy to rationalize that things would get better.

After our daughter was born, things were back to happy, at first. But as we came up on her first birthday, my husband was becoming manipulative again. As I look back, I realize his manipulation was very covert. I just did not realize what was going on.

When I look back at the stumbling blocks that I just climbed over or did the limbo under during the infertility trials I often wonder if God was warning me to pull up stakes and run for my life. God knew I would never leave my children if I had any. I would endure anything for my children. But when I look back, I also remember a man that for a time was brilliant, kind, and loving. The Dr. Jekyll and Mr. Hyde act was not every day. There were moments of bliss that reminded me of why I fell in love with him, like the time he took us out for my first Mother's Day. We drove through the mountains, stopping at small towns along the way for little sightseeing walks. It was something he had planned on his own. A very simple day, just what I wanted, only the three of us with no one else around. I remember the light in his blue eyes and the calm in his face. What I did not know at the time was it would be a rare occasion to see his face like that ever again. It was shortly after that day that my husband began to drink more than socially, or at least I began to notice that it was more than socially.

If I had to put a finger on what role I played in the stumbling block God gave me during those years, it would have to be blindness. I simply did not want to see the forest or the trees let alone any road signs God was putting before me. Many people ask had I known the future if I would have done something differently at that point. I would have to say I would have. I would have dealt with the manipulation and lying differently.

I did not realize there was a game being played back then, and I was just a card from the deck. Blindness was a big stumbling block and I had to learn even people you love can be dishonest. It even states this in the Bible.

> Do not be deceived: "Bad Company ruins good morals." (1 Cor 15:33–34)[3]

During my daughter's first two years of life, my blindness was lifted. My husband began drinking with the neighbor across the street around that time. The neighbor had installed a bar in his basement. It was quite a setup. My husband would take our daughter over while I was out running errands. She would sit on the floor and play while they drank. It was at this time the drinking became bad; it was all out in the open, around me all the time. It was not just a habit you could pass off; it was real abuse. It was falling-down drunk, loud yelling, and demeaning comments. I could see the problem and vocalize that it was a problem. My husband honestly said he would stop. I believed him. Unfortunately, the neighbor across the street became his best friend. Drinking events were plentiful.

Soon it became time to use the embryos that were left over from our first in vitro fertilization procedure. As we fought about the amount of drinking my husband was doing, I worried about my age and the success chances of the frozen embryos. I was not young. I begged my husband to let us get started on the second implantation when my daughter was a year old. However, my husband put conditions on the implantation. In order to complete the next round of in vitro procedures and to implant the frozen embryos for our second child, my husband required that I complete my PhD. This degree was something I had started before we met. I thought he was concerned that I would never finish after I had two kids. I would be too content being a mom.

Having all the coursework completed and most of the dissertation, I did not have much more to do on the degree anyway. I finished my dissertation in six weeks' time and graduated shortly before Christmas. I was pregnant using our frozen embryos by January. This pregnancy was different, though. My husband and I were not a team of husband and wife. We were two totally different teams. The first team was a team of two, my daughter and me. The second team was a team of three: my husband, the man across the street, and his wife. When I went to the doctor's office to see if there was a beating heart for the first time, I went with my daughter. My husband was in Las Vegas on a vacation with the guy across the street.

There was a great deal of drinking and gambling. When I called to talk about the doctor's visit, I reached an incoherent husband who was not concerned about the heartbeat at all. Out of spite, I told him that all the embryos took, and I was pregnant with triplets. When I informed him we would need a minivan, he sobered up really quick. I jokingly came clean and gave him the truth which resulted in laughter from both of us.

This new team structure made the second pregnancy different, though. Physically I was covered; the doctors knew up front I was going to be a high-risk patient. They made sure they had a cerclage in place a soon as possible. Those were stitches through the cervix, so it did not open. Once those stitches were in place, I was fairly self-sufficient. However, being pregnant, taking care of a two-year-old, and contending with this new family dynamic was exhausting. Sometimes, when my daughter and I would take a nap, I would wake up and my daughter would be at the neighbor's, surrounded by adults who were intoxicated. I was condemned for not thinking this was normal. I could not believe how my husband was falling prey to this asinine behavior. He was a smart and caring man. So caring that once my husband even stated he was trying to convince them to come to church with us.

Were they using his compassion against him? What was the draw?

There were nights that he would not come home until two or three in the morning and think nothing of it. Once he even carried a loaded gun home and said, "I need this to protect our house. He gave it to me as a gift." I told him to give it back—and I was thankful that he listened.

As the terrible family dynamics continued to heat up, halfway during the pregnancy it was determined our new baby did not have fully developing kidneys. It was undetermined whether the baby would live without a kidney transplant upon birth. There was even a time when they were considering in utero surgery. I spent much of my pregnancy in doctor's offices with our daughter in tow. I merely informed my husband of our progress.

My husband seemed unconcerned for our welfare. His stance was we had great insurance and I would figure out how to make it work in our favor. I remember so many caring nurses reading to my daughter while we waited for countless specialists. Many took her for walks outside whatever exam room I was in. I longed for family close by or friends who didn't work to lend a hand. However, that was not the hand I was dealt, so my two-year-old daughter and I just kept pushing forward.

The last straw was during my birthday that year. My husband decided to play in a golf tournament on my birthday. His reasoning was he had never missed one in all the years of the tournament's existence. The guy across the street was on his team, of course. The kicker was that I was seven months pregnant and finally put on bed rest for the remainder of the pregnancy. The baby was not making amniotic fluid, and to conserve what was left, I was to move only in dire circumstances.

My husband said five hours would OK for me to be home alone with our daughter. He left us in bed with a couple of movies to watch together and some snacks, figuring between the movies, snacks, and nap time he had enough time to play the course. When eight hours had passed I got up carrying her and cooked dinner. Shortly after, my husband, his sidekick, and the sidekick's wife came in. The wife took my child without even asking, leaving for her house across the street. Then her drunk husband put my even drunker husband in bed and said he needed to stay there. I was livid. I called the wife on the phone and told her to bring my baby back or I was calling the police. I told her husband that I was the one on bed rest and that I did not want to see him in my home anymore.

Immediately after I had my daughter back, we drove to mass. It was Saturday night, and I knew I needed some sort of spiritual relief. By the time I returned, my husband was in the tub, stating he would never get that out of control again and begging me not to leave him. I believed he had hit rock bottom and saw the error of his ways.

The next day I saw blood spotting when I went to the bathroom. I arranged for a doctor's visit, and my daughter and I went in for an ultrasound. This is when I was informed that my movement used up all the fluid surrounding the baby, and he was not making any more. We were being admitted into the hospital for an emergency delivery if things did not change quickly. I called a friend, who took a couple of days off from work to watch my daughter. We met in the hospital room. Over the next few days, they watched the baby's progress closely but determined there was no hope of regaining enough fluid to make it to nine months. Because of the activity from tournament incident, our son was born two months early.

Once he was delivered, the specialists examined his kidneys and determined one would need to be removed, and the remaining one was having issues due to kinks in the ureter. He spent two weeks in the neonatal unit with specialists coming in and out. Thankfully, we were released with a surgery date to be named later for the kidney removal.

It was at this time that I stopped seeing my husband get drunk. I did not stop seeing him drink, but he did not drink to excess in my presence. He and I agreed he could have two drinks per day, period. He was back to being the man I married, the man I loved for a long time. We were happy. I did my volunteer work and added some community college teaching on the side, and he held down an incredible job. Eight months later, we had my son's nonfunctioning kidney removed, and life motored on.

So how did God use this terrible time to mold me into who I am today? I did not realize it at the time, but I think God was proving to me that I had no boundaries.

As the situation stood at that time, I was self-sufficient and could deal with a multitude of stressful situations at once. I could arrange the logistics of meals and naps for a one-year-old, doctor's appointments for a high-risk pregnancy, keep a clean house and yard, and get dinner on the table by 5:30 p.m. Plus, I was involved in a host of volunteer efforts for our church. If I could do all of that, I thought, *Why shouldn't I?*

I truly felt it was my job to take care of all the medical issues for the pregnancy as well as take care of my daughter by myself. I also took care of my son's medical needs after he was born. I was strong and self-sufficient. Since I didn't have a full-time job outside of the home, I believed that my husband should have his free time to de-stress from work. However, this thought process proved to be a stumbling block. When I think about it now, by taking care of everything, he had no duties other than shouting orders.

My husband had all the fun, and I had all the stress. I did the dirty work. I inadvertently allowed my husband to think he was infallible. If there was an unpleasant household chore and I was sick, the chore did not get done. If something needed to be returned to a store, whether I purchased it or not, I was the one to take it back. If bad news needed to be broken to a family member, I made the call. By not requiring my husband to shoulder some of the unpleasant tasks, I had no boundaries for how I was to be treated. It was not long before I had reduced myself to a servant to my husband instead of an equal partner in our marriage.

Having no boundaries became an issue when the drinking became out of control. I should have left. However, I pleaded, yelled, and was generally disillusioned instead. Maybe if I had been more forceful and just left, my husband would have listened.

I say "maybe" because with alcoholism, the need to drink gets stronger as time goes on. It is hard to say when each alcoholic reaches the point of no return, and they cannot change. Mind you, I do not blame myself for his alcoholism. But I cannot help but wonder if I had stronger boundaries from the beginning if the situation would have been different. Would he have been scared of losing us? Would he have wanted to quit drinking altogether instead of just having a few drinks in my presence?

I was no longer blind, but I was too capable for my own good. No boundaries were my stumbling block in this period. What was worse, was since there were no boundaries from the beginning, there was no hope of creating them after time went on.

CHAPTER 3

Addiction Is an Accident That Happens When You Are Searching for Happiness[4]

—Stefan Klein, PhD

What sorrow for those who say that evil is good and good is evil, that dark is light and light is dark, that bitter is sweet and sweet is bitter. What sorrow for those who are wise in their own eyes and think themselves so clever. What sorrow for those who are heroes at drinking wine and boast about all the alcohol they can hold. They take bribes to let the wicked go free, and they punish the innocent. (Is 5:20–23)[5]

My husband's manipulative behavior became worse after our eight-month-old son had kidney surgery. He would lie about conversations he had with people about me. He would state that everyone around me thought I was mean and cold, and that I was a terrible parent. When I would try to defend myself with those people, they thought I was silly, stating they would never say stuff like that.

With all the lying, it took me awhile to figure out it was alcohol that was still the issue. I was still only seeing him have two drinks a day, usually red wine.

Many would consider the fact that I never knew my husband was getting drunk odd. But at this time in my life, I was knee-deep in massive volunteer events for three different parishes, holding down two part-time jobs, and toting two very young children around everywhere I went. I was the "Do it all mom." I was on committees that put together volunteer events for more than a hundred families. At my home parish, I was the director of children's liturgy, writing and delivering children's services for three masses.

Many families at least attend church together each Sunday; however, I never even saw my husband on Sundays. There were seventy-five families I was keeping track of. I left the house after I fixed breakfast for my kids so I could be at church to teach the 8:30 a.m. religious education classes. My husband would arrive to drop off the kids for the 10:00 a.m. religious education class, then he would proceed to the church to usher for that mass. The kids and I would then stay for the 11:30 a.m. segment of classes while my husband would run errands. I would even serve the kids lunch at the church because it was just "easier."

I saw my husband on Sundays early in the morning before I left for mass, then late in the afternoon when he returned home from running errands. I did not see him in the middle when he dropped the kids off. In the beginning, when my kids were young, my husband would leave them with a volunteer. As the years wore on, my husband just shooed them in the door as he went to usher at mass, and they found their way from there. My kids knew where to go in the building; they were there every Sunday, plus numerous times through the week.

The times my kids and I were away from my husband were plentiful. I did not monitor him for anything. He said he would stop drinking heavily after the incident at my son's birth, and I believed him. But over time, I began to wonder about my husband's health. Mind you, I did not know he was drinking heavily again. I would just see him sweat profusely, have mood swings that were unbelievable, and start having difficulty seeing. His hands started having tremors.

There were times I would come home from working one of my part-time jobs and the kids would be playing with each other on the floor while their dad was asleep. I could not wake him up, not by shouting or shaking him. When I think about it now, I could kick myself for being so naive, but I had never been in the presence of a functional alcoholic, someone who could hold down a great job while drinking like a fish.

It was a very scary time. I would ask my friends what they thought was occurring, and one stated that he was probably passed out because of alcoholism. I defended my husband by stating I never saw any bottles, and only saw him drink two glasses of wine after work. When that close friend stated he could be hiding his drinking, disposing of the bottles, I began to look evidence and found none.

That is when I started to look for something more medical.

I began pushing my husband toward doctors. We had had our general practitioner for a quite a while, so I was comfortable about speaking to her about my husband's ailments. When she ran tests and did not find anything, I was even more concerned. I could see physical problems. What I did not know was that my husband was going into the appointments stating that he was fine, and that I was making up stories because I had nothing better to do. The doctor was kind enough to run a variety of tests, each proving nothing. In the end, she recommended that during the next episode that I call 911, or somehow get my husband to the emergency room. Then she terminated herself from being our doctor.

I took the statement to call 911 during the next episode to heart. I planned for the next time. I knew my neighbor was studying to be a nurse, so I talked to him. He gave me his schedule and said just to give him a call.

One Saturday when I arrived home from a part-time job, my husband was asleep on the couch, and I could not wake him. I thought about calling an ambulance, but I did not want to worry the kids. But my neighbor next door was home. I walked over and told him what was going on.

When we walked back in the house, my husband was up and very disoriented and speeding out of the driveway.

I talked with my neighbor anyway, and oddly enough, my husband stumbled in the door after a few moments. My neighbor agreed that my husband needed to go to the emergency room, stating he would stay with the kids. My husband was despondent, but he got in the car. When we arrived, knowing we were going to sit in the waiting room for a good while, I made them take a urine sample as soon as we walked in the door. As time progressed, my husband got better and clearer. By the time we were taken back into the room, he was bound to prove me wrong—that there was nothing wrong with him.

It was a shock when they drew blood and found a blood alcohol level of 0.352. Even after all that time had passed, from the couch at home to the hospital bed, he still had a blood alcohol level of 0.352.

That day I found out a great deal. I found out that my husband was an alcoholic. I learned that my husband had drunk a pitcher of margaritas that morning after I had left for my part-time job, and that his trip prior to us leaving for the hospital was to throw away the evidence. I also found out that he did that every Saturday and Sunday when I left for any reason. At that moment, I learned that he was drunk while he ushered in church every Sunday while I was teaching religious education at the 10:00 a.m. mass. In addition, he drove drunk when he brought the kids to church to meet me for the religious education.

On that day at the emergency room, I learned that for years my husband drank while he ran errands, whether he had the kids in the car or not. I learned that when he took the kids to school in the morning, he would throw away the empty wine and liquor bottles in the vacant field at the edge of the subdivision. Finally, I learned that my now seven-year-old daughter was getting up in the middle of the night looking for cans and bottles to put in the car to be gotten rid of. In retrospect, I could now see why I should be grateful to God—my children had been on their own in the house every time that I left them in my husband's care. He was too busy getting intoxicated. I was grateful that they were never harmed from him drinking and driving. Both kids were safe because of God's grace.

On the way home from the hospital, my husband stated he knew he had a problem and that he needed time to take care for it. I loved him and my kids, so I agreed to give him time to explore treatment options. What I did not remember was my husband lied about everything, even the smallest things that really did not matter.

I began our life again, hoping to keep things normal. We had a trip planned to see my family in Michigan a few days after the emergency room visit. It was an annual trip. I began to pack, wondering what I would say to my parents when I arrived. Would they be condescending, would they be compassionate, or would they even care that there was a serious issue at hand? I couldn't tell what the outcome would be; we were not close.

The night prior to leaving, my husband went into our seven-year-old daughter's room and hit her. There was no provocation—she was sleeping. I was packing and happened to be walking through the hall when I saw the whole thing. She woke up and started crying. She was scared and hurting. As I was calming her down, I could see that he was visibly drunk.

I knew it was time for me to get reinforcements to help him see that he needed help to address his drinking problem. I called my husband's mother, telling her about the emergency room visit and events of the evening, asking her to help her son get treatment. She listened and said that she would talk with him, but the result was still the same. My husband still wanted to try Alcoholics Anonymous (AA) before anything else.

It was a long ride to Michigan the next day. He begged me not to discuss this with my parents. However, I needed some sort of guidance, and I hoped my parents could at least point me in the right direction. Unfortunately, my parents plainly stated it was my issue to deal with. They did not want to be involved in any way.

Oh, how the stumbling blocks that I had built up came tumbling down! I was tripping all over them. My husband could not have just two drinks. He could not stop at two; he hid the rest. I just wasn't savvy enough to catch him. My children suffered when they were in his presence through no fault of their own. My family did not want to be involved, and his barely acted. One relative said, "You can handle this; you handle everything else. Why should we get involved?" There was no sugar-coating this. I was alone. I had built an image of a self-sufficient woman. By believing in my husband that he could manage having only two drinks, and by not looking into what alcoholism looked like instead of what I thought it looked like, I managed to miss all the signs. I allowed it to continue right under my nose.

I was alone and very angry about it. No one was helping me with this terrible predicament. I was on a one-woman mission to get people to help me to address this issue. What I did not realize was that God was using this issue to make me useful to others, someday ... a long way off. But for now, I was to struggle desperately—physically, emotionally, financially, and spiritually for years to come. I was alone and angry about it. My newest stumbling block was anger. Anger at myself for being so ignorant. Anger at my husband for being so mean. Anger at my family for not helping and at his for continuing to ignore the problem. Anger at the people around me for not getting involved.

CHAPTER 4

You Don't Change Because Things Come in Your Life. You Get Better Because Things Come in Your Life[6]

—Wayman Tisdale

Throughout your life you will face situations that are completely out of your control. These situations will force you to make a decision to abandon God or worship him in the midst of the situations that are happening. However, if you do not remember God's past faithfulness, you will have a difficult time of trusting him when you are up against the wall. Mainly because adversity introduces man to himself, it is then that we realize that we are just human.[7]
—Pete Wilson

Now what should I do?

When we returned home to Tennessee, our lives did not stop just because dad had a drinking problem. He wanted to address the problem on his own terms, and I wanted to make sure the kids had as normal a life as possible. And with spring fast approaching, there were a great deal of kids' activities to maneuver.

Our daughter was in soccer and Girl Scouts and our son was in baseball. I had committed to being the troop leader for our daughter and the dugout coach for our son. Being the do-it-all mom, I had gotten used to transporting the kids to their events by myself, as well as keeping the household going. So, like any do-it-all mom does, I put on my happy face and motored on. I was committed to keeping the kids' lives as normal as possible.

The only tasks my husband needed to worry about were keeping a job and going to AA to address his sobriety. I wanted to give him his time to try it his way. I would check him before he left, and he would be fine. When he would come home, he seemed to be doing fine. He had no smell about him, he wasn't sweating or shaking, he never slurred his words. He said he was going to AA and getting things worked out. I felt like he had turned the corner, and he really was trying to be involved in the kids' activities.

That's when I started to let him take the kids to a few events here and there.

However, my husband dabbled in AA for a short time while he juggled going to all the kids' activities. I think he felt the need to keep up the appearance that nothing was wrong. I know he felt that he could stop drinking at any time; he just went to AA to appease me. He stated that several times. To me this meant his commitment to AA was not strong from the start. He felt he was in control of his drinking. I began to feel like I was now dealing with a man who had no boundaries in our married life, and what was worse, the alcohol had taken over his rational mind.

By the middle of baseball season, my husband was back to drinking and driving without my knowledge. That's when I realized we had not turned a corner; he had just become craftier and more selective about his drinking. Unfortunately, the excessive drinking became apparent when I was getting ready to attend a Girl Scout function and my husband was to take our son to baseball for team pictures. They had left in plenty of time to make the scheduled time slot, and I had watched them leave, so I knew he was sober. However, I received a call shortly before I was to leave with my daughter for the Girl Scout event. My son and husband had not arrived for the pictures. I finagled a ride for my daughter and passed off my leader duties in minutes. As soon as I did, I received a call from another mother on the team. My husband had finally arrived, drunk. Her call was to inform me that if I did not show up by the time pictures were over the department of human services was going to be called to pick up my son. I was also politely informed that I would be put in jail for child endangerment.

I was shocked. I was to blame, not my husband, who had been drinking all the way from the house to the ball field, plus stopped in a parking lot before getting to the ball field to finish the bottle of liquor. If words were spoken to him, I will never know. I arrived shortly before the pictures were taken. Everyone went about their business like nothing was ever said. My husband scurried off to parts unknown. When my son and I returned home he was nowhere to be found.

This event marked a turning point in our lives. It was at that time that the manipulative behavior of my husband turned into verbal and physical abuse. His lying was paramount in the relationship, but it was dwarfed by his anger. During the next three years this abuse was blatant at home but not in public. But as a Christian I was taught to forgive and try to help those who are in need. That's what I resolved to do. I tried desperately to hold my family together and keep the kids from seeing any signs of abuse. I kept them involved in all sorts or activities away from the house.

As I tried to keep the kids from seeing my husband's anger, our happiness became truly compartmentalized. We had a separate life when their dad was away. We painted, played games, went to parks, and ran through water hoses. When he was home, it was a different story. If the kids were reading or playing and their dad became loud, I would move them. If he was upset about something, I would fix it. If he wanted to do something, we did it. Whatever it took to keep their dad happy, that is what we did. I had become a passive person for the sake of the kids' peace of mind. There was no way of communicating anything to my husband about his drinking. I asked my mother-in-law to speak to him again. It was at that time that I found out she had not spoken to him in the beginning. She had passed off the task to her husband, someone no one liked or respected, not even his own children.

The anger and abuse circled back to a period of calmness many times, though, so I really felt he was working on his sobriety. However, those times were followed by my husband trying to prove to me that he could stop after two drinks. The proving ground was very pronounced. He would proclaim his ability to control his drinking to everyone if we were out socially. He would say, "My wife says I can only have two, so please do not fill my glass" or "See, you're the one with the problem—you make me want to drink, and I can only have two." When my husband felt he had made his point to everyone including me, his drinking habits went back to the old routine. He would drink whenever he was driving or when no one was looking. Each time he reverted, the drinking became worse, and the abuse was more pronounced. When the alcoholism became readily apparent to everyone publicly, normalcy in our lives had long been gone.

My happiness revolved around my children during this time. I made clothes for them, read to them, and did everything a stay-at-home mom with part-time jobs could do. It was easy to compartmentalize my life, keeping my husband's problems segmented to the period between 5:00 p.m. and 9:00 p.m. Thinking back, I can see how I had two separate lives—the happy stay-at-home mom from morning until 5:00 p.m., then the stressed, protective witch from 5:00 p.m. until bedtime.

How could a loving God be so cruel? I thought.

I was determined to make the best of it and try to learn what God was teaching. However, what stumbling block could I have possibly conjured up? I was not blind to the drinking or the abuse after the baseball incident. I was trying to keep the marriage together and allow my husband time to get help, which I thought was the Christian thing to do. The only thing that I can think of that might be a possibility would be my ability to analyze a situation outwardly, but not inwardly.

I never thought of how anything affected me inwardly. I never looked at what was happening to my soul.

I dealt with God on the surface, taking life at face value, but never looking deeper. I did not know there was a "deeper."

Looking back, I can mark how our family life deteriorated by the Disney vacations we took.

We made a trip each year, and each year's trip was different. Everything appeared to the outsider as though our family was leading a wonderful life. My husband would plan every detail—where we went, stayed, and ate. When the children and I would go to sleep in the hotel room, he would stay wake and go to the lobby to sort out our plans for the next day. It was very sweet.

With the limited number of places to drink on the property, the drinking was kept to a minimum. However, during our first trip after our son was born, there was an incident while we were at Epcot, the only place in Disney that served alcohol. My husband left us at a fountain, coming back drunk three hours. We ended up in a huge fight; I took the kids back to the hotel on the Disney bus line. The next year's trip was a different story. The drinking event occurred when we went out to dinner off the property. My husband became so drunk that I left him at the restaurant and drove back to the hotel, leaving him to take a cab.

During our final trip it was much worse. We stayed on-site, and my husband went to the hotel bar when we were asleep. On our last night, he became so drunk he couldn't find his way back to the room. Six security guards brought him in while we were asleep and threw him on the bed. I woke up in the middle of the ruckus. The next day he merely blew off the fact that he had mistakenly went to the wrong hotel room drunk and caused a scene at the Disney Resort. In addition, he stated it wasn't his fault, but mine—I went to bed too early. He could not stay up and read in bed and reading in the bathroom had become too uncomfortable. Thankfully, the kids didn't remember security bringing him into the hotel room drunk. They were asleep, exhausted from a week of fun.

When I look back on this time of my life to try and figure out how God was trying to develop me into what would be useful to him, I am still at a great loss for words. The abuse was debilitating. More importantly, the people around me who were my friends never came forward to set the record straight. Neither family, mine nor his, offered to help. The lack of support only served to cement the terrible image that my husband had painted in my mind. I felt worthless and mean. I somehow deserved this terrible mess that my children and I were in.

But to be useful to God, I had to go through this stretch of time. I had to be abandoned. I had to be beaten. I had to be the lone protector of my children while the people in my world played and had carefree fun. I had to solider on alone no matter how many times I asked for help and was turned away casually, with "Oh, you'll figure it out," or "It's your job as the wife, not mine," or "I have to work," or so many other one-liners.

CHAPTER 5

Surrendering Your Opinions Leads to Surrendering Your Self-Image

The very purpose of existence is to reconcile the glowing opinion we have of ourselves with the appalling things that other people think about us.[8]
—Quentin Crisp

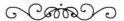

When I found that no one wanted to help me deal with this terrible family issue, I started to search for any type of reason this insanity was happening. I read books like I was cramming for a final exam. I read everything about topics ranging from alcoholism to dealing with personality disorders. I had a healthy list of religious self-help books as well. Through this self-education process, I found that I had a huge stumbling block that I did not even know about.

My newly found stumbling block was that I changed how I felt about things.

It did not matter what my mind was changing about. My thoughts about current events or my thoughts on what to serve for dinner changed based on who I was talking to.

When I started noticing this occurring, I found the pattern wasn't excluded to just daily events. I also changed the thoughts about myself. Thoughts on how I should feel, if I was correct, what I should do next—and let's not forget what I should think about myself. Every thought I had changed based on who I was talking to.

I used to be a decisive person, but now whenever I was around someone who spoke with confidence, my mind changed on how I felt. My opinion swayed to theirs. It did not matter if they were right or wrong. I assumed I was always wrong. My self-education books helped me realize that I had a problem with self-esteem and self-doubt.

The abuse had taken its toll.

The self-reliant, self-assured person was there on the outside, but inside there was nothing. I was someone who didn't think, plan, or feel. I just existed, going from one day to the next. My to-do list was long, and it kept me from realizing how empty I had become. Outside, it still appeared to everyone that I had the alcoholic recovery plan under control, I am sure. But the reality was that I was on a journey to find my soul.

Once I realized what I was doing, I began to watch myself and my reactions. In doing so, I noticed the same phenomenon of swaying opinions with some other people around me. I hung around the same volunteer crowd; we were involved in multiple events at different parishes, so it was easy to monitor reactions of people and see patterns emerge.

I noticed how some of us in our quiet corner did not really have our own opinions, or if we did, as a group we gravitated toward the beliefs held by someone who showed confidence. Was it possible that our little corner of people was a group that did not believe in ourselves yet believed everything else? When I think back, some of our ideas were pretty good, but the thoughts never were voiced to the larger group.

When I took a look at some of the ideas that were thrown around the larger volunteer group, the opinions ranged from what to do at our functions to more judgmental topics on who should be doing what and for whom. And let's not forget the pious opinions about situations in various parishes that we were helping.

Many times, those opinions were very far from the truth; however, we still believed them.

I found the whole process ironic. Isn't that what we all want? To understand the truth? Yet we never looked at how we formed our thoughts, where the information came from, or what the motives were for the people doling out the information. Opinions swayed to the people who seemed to be the surest of themselves.

When we form an opinion and make our up minds, we are supposed to weigh all the sides beforehand. So how do we know we have a problem with changing our opinions? A key sign is consistency. We have an issue when we start *consistently* surrendering our own beliefs for those of others around us. Typically, there is a balance between keeping our own opinion and changing it. Consistently changing our opinion without examining the facts marks that maybe our self-esteem needs some shoring up. Surrendering our beliefs on a regular basis should be a sign to us that we need to search our own *internal situation* for the truth. We need to start asking ourselves questions.

The first questions we should ask ourselves is *Why do I doubt my ability to make a sound opinion?* and we should follow it with *Just why do I give in to others on a regular basis?* Another set of questions to bring in some valuable information is *Am I uneducated about the events around me? Or do I doubt our self-worth?* And finally, another worthy question is *Am I ignoring the motives of the people that I have surrounded myself with?* I know that should have been one that I asked myself.

I had no balance in how I looked at situations around me. Everyone else was in the "better" category, and I was in the "not" category. I wish I would have thought of these questions when I was doing my soul searching. I was as far over in the "not" category as I could get. I could not weigh the good and bad in any situation.

My self-esteem surely needed shoring up; it needed a complete overhaul. I had no beliefs of my own and it did not matter what the topic was. Not having an ability to balance out my thoughts was a big stumbling block for me.

To get a balanced perspective, I started to look at both sides of any situation or conversation. I found that sometimes the person that I was talking to never considered someone else's version of the truth. I started to ask myself more questions then, like *Are they so educated about this that they have all the answers?* and *Why do they think that others who come from a different environment might not have a different view that will lead to a better solution?* And let's not forget the big question *Are they really that arrogant that that believe they are always right?* I thought of the old saying, "Pride goes before the fall." Maybe in those situations we are our own stumbling block. I thought that I was never right, so I knew that was not my issue.

During this examination, I found my husband thought he was *always right*. But I just did not have enough self-esteem to understand at the time what was going on. I needed to continue with my self-help books and have a long, soul-searching talk with God.

Unfortunately, a prayerful conversation and a quick answer about our souls do not usually go together. For that quick, soul-boosting fix, we ask the questions of our close friends and family. Questions come out of our mouths like "Do you believe what others think about me?" Or "Is it right to behave like that?" When we get the answer we want to hear, we stop looking for the truth. We do not begin to ask the hard questions of ourselves.

This is the start of becoming our own growth-stunted stumbling block. When we do not ask the tough questions of ourselves and only follow what people around us think, it can lead to surrendering our own opinion.

When are having the heart-to-heart conversation with God, we have to be prepared for a time lag. When we are having this conversation, we have no way of quickly validating the answers. That can be a stumbling block, too. We are not patient or cannot see or hear God's answer. Between the waiting and the recognizing, we as humans lose focus on the bigger picture. I know I lost focus many times as I was waiting and praying and crying. I went back to riding on the quick-fix merry-go-round several times. Eventually, I would hear whispers from my soul saying *What are you doing? You know better than that.* Slowly I would hit my knees again, praying for more answers.

Any conversation between us humans and God is a process that takes trust that He is listening and will respond in His time. But waiting is hard to do when you already have a compromised self-image. It is even harder when the people you have surrounded yourself with are adding to your personal doubts. However, if done thoroughly, the soul searching should lead to a deeper relationship with God.

After all, who should we really ask about our souls?

If we wait and pray long enough, sometimes there is a beginning of a conversation that makes us sit up and take notice of the truth of opinions and motivations. Like a light bulb turning on to reality, and you say to yourself *Oh, how could I be so dumb? I know what is going on here.*

This light bulb flicked on in my yard when I was giving our dog a haircut one day. When that light bulb went off, I realized just how many times I gave in to my husband's opinion.

When our daughter was five, we found a puppy on the interstate. I had always wanted a dog for the kids, and they we old enough to enjoy one. My husband was apprehensive, and the puppy was taken by a young couple who had also stopped. We did exchange numbers in case they could not find a home for it. Two weeks later, a call came, and we picked up our Lucky to bring her home. She was small and black. We did not have a fenced in yard, so I rigged up a dog run with the help of a neighbor. She was great from the start, spending the day outside and the night in our bed.

As she grew, she developed a few white patches. Once when she was full grown, I was outside playing with her and noticed her underside was reddish brown in places. When I casually brought it up to my husband, he stated that she had not changed colors. It was dirt, and the dog needed a bath. With our clay dirt, that seemed plausible, so I scrubbed the dog down. However, the reddish brown remained. My husband stated the clay had dyed her fur. Not growing up with clay dirt, I assumed he must know what he was talking about. Why would anyone be so adamant about the color of a dog? Years later we started shaving Lucky because of the heat in the summer. What did

I find underneath? A black dog with white spots under her chin and reddish-brown spots on her underside. I was amazed at myself and how easily that I accepted my husband's version. I was equally amazed at how my husband could not conceive of anything being different from his opinion.

It took shaving the dog and finding the brown spots underneath her thick, black fur to make me realize that my opinion mattered. I remember sitting in the yard feeling like I had just a bit of my self-esteem back. I realized I needed to look at my husband's statements just a little more closely. When I did, I began to see a pattern. It was a sign of things to come. Whatever the situation, my husband and I were on opposite sides of it. If I brought something up first, my husband's opinion was immediately the exact opposite.

My husband's opinions went from small, insignificant statements of fact about everyday mishaps to saying I was the reason everything happened. Slowly, I became the root of all evil. If the light bulbs went out, it was my fault they did not get changed. If the grass was too long, it was my fault that we had a push mower instead of a rider. When I bought a riding lawn mower, it was my fault that my husband did not get any exercise. It was my fault that we had no money; I did not have a full-time job. However, I could not look for a job that made less than $40,000 because I would have to pay for day care. There was not one thing that my husband considered a "no fault" situation. Looking back, I could recognize how finding those brown spots gave me confidence to stand up for myself. I knew the truth all along, but just did not trust in my opinion to state it. I had become passive, afraid of the fallout from my husband's temper. I no longer cared how he made me look or feel. The only thing that mattered to me was that there was not any anger for the kids to be around. What I did not realize is that my husband was just using the anger and the differing opinions to get his way. Right there in the yard, I figured out how to turn a stumbling block into a cornerstone for growth.

CHAPTER 6

Better a Patient Man than a Warrior, a Man Who Controls His Temper than One Who Takes a City
(Prv 16:32)[9]

> Don't say anything that would hurt another person. Instead, speak only what is good so that you can give help whenever it is needed. That way, what you say will help those who hear you. (Eph 4:29 GWT) [10]

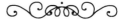

It was a devastating time of my life. I was abandoned by my friends; they were tired of dealing our family dynamics. My husband's family refused to get involved, stating it was my job to get my husband sober. My family stated my husband was my problem to deal with, and that if I were nicer to him, he wouldn't need to drink. I was truly alone with two small children depending on me to figure a way out of this misery. So just how do you deal with a manipulative person, and what is the best practice?

If bad company ruins good morals, it would seem that the best solution is to stay away from the person. But what if the person with the unacceptable behavior is a family member? What then? What do you do with a person who has total control over your life who is lying and manipulating all the events around you? How do you react?

Scripture says you should be *patient and not a warrior.*

The manipulative mind of my husband became clear at the fiftieth wedding anniversary of my husband's parents. The events will always make me wonder about the "patient versus warrior" concept. With my husband failing at sobriety, I was not excited about getting together with his family. Everyone brought multiple types of alcoholic beverages.

During the weekend event, there were many errands to run to pick up items for the anniversary party. Since I knew he went off drinking on the sly using errands as his cover, I made the comment to make sure someone "smelled his breath" when he returned. The comment enraged his family.

The result was a black mark against me; I was shunned all weekend. But something else occurred. My husband made an astounding announcement to me. He said, "You achieved in one sentence what I could not do all these years. You finally made my family realize that you are awful. For the first time in my life, my family believes and supports me." I thought, *What exactly has my husband been telling them during our marriage? Why can't they see he drinks heavily in their presence?*

As I look back in time, I often wonder if this is where my deep-seated anger is from. My husband always managed to manipulate what people thought of me, and I always felt like I had to clear up details. It made me angry that people could not tell what the truth was, and I was always trying to defend myself or prove something. When I think about it, I helped cement the image he conjured up by getting angry and ranting about him. If I had learned to stand back, saying nothing and letting the events unfold, would the result have been the same? Would people have seen my husband as a manipulative alcoholic and me as the victim?

Many competent women would find this thought pattern just as manipulative and demeaning as the behavior of my husband. But what is manipulative about letting someone reap what they sow? By allowing my husband to feel the distaste that others had for out-of-control drinking, I may have saved myself some grief. However, I was too concerned with how people viewed me and how I was solving the problem. I did not realize then that the only one who needed to know the truth already knew everything. God was the only one I needed to impress. He was probably unimpressed with my yelling and screaming.

God already knew about the drinking and the lying. I did not need to prove or clear up anything. The following passage is clear on that point.

> Do not be deceived: God is not mocked, for whatever one sows that will he also reap. For the one who sows to his own flesh will from the flesh reap corruption, but the one who sows to the Spirit will from the Spirit reap eternal life. (Gal 6:7–8 ESV)[11]

The way I handled the situation was by trying to be an active player fighting for change. I plainly pointed out the drinking problem as well as the family and friends who allowed it to continue. I did not care about the abuse that would happen behind closed doors; it was going to happen anyway. However, this "active player" behavior was getting in the way of God doing his work. By being vocal and stating the truth in no uncertain terms, I looked like a strong, capable woman. The flipside to this is that strong, capable women also are seen as catty and hard. My husband used this to invent a cause for his drinking. Since I was not compassionate to his alcoholic situation, I was the cause of it. My husband blamed me for his drinking, setting himself up as the victim.

But for me to have acted differently I needed an understanding of how God was trying to work within the situation. I needed to learn how God uses situations to teach lessons to everyone involved. Looking back, my way of speaking up was my way of keeping my self-worth. However now, looking at the proverb:

> Better a patient man than a warrior, a man who controls his temper than one who takes a city. (Prv 16:32)[12]

I can see how I helped the events unfold as they did. Sometimes the quiet patient man can look to others and ask just what exactly he can do. These quiet, patient people receive help.

I was just the opposite. I was becoming a strong, vocal woman on the outside, even though I was not really confident on the inside. But regardless of how you feel on the inside, women who act strong and competent are expected to "do" and "fix things." They are asked, "Why isn't this taken care of?" not "How can I help you?" By appearing strong and capable, I was giving everyone around me an excuse not to get involved.

It took a closer walk with God to help me understand how I was being manipulated here on earth. I was part of my own manipulation problem. It took examining my soul with God to find my strength was my stumbling block. But it was the soul examination that began to put me back on track.

Being patient and alone is hard when you and your children are in danger with no hope of getting out. You need to be someone who is quietly plotting an escape. You need to be someone who can manage conflict resolution. You need to be a *patient warrior*.

CHAPTER 7

The Pain You Feel Today Is the Strength You Feel Tomorrow. For Every Challenge Encountered, There Is Opportunity for Growth

—Unknown

Knowledge is acquired by seeking it, and patience is acquiring by striving to be patient. The one who strives to attain good will be given it, and the one who strives to protect himself from evil will be protected.

—Unknown

I am convinced that anyone can become a patient warrior. It's like playing chess. The first step is to use the most effective and healthiest form of communication—an assertive style but not aggressive. Believe it or not, being assertive is how we naturally express ourselves when our self-esteem is intact, giving us the confidence to communicate without games and manipulation. When we communicate our needs clearly and forthrightly, we know our limits and refuse to be pushed beyond them just because someone else wants or needs something different from us. So, what goes wrong?

We are usually met with the stumbling blocks of people who do not want to hear what we have to say.

Recognizing how you are being talked to by others is the second step of becoming a patient warrior. I learned to recognize the other communication types—aggressive, passive, or passive-aggressive—when I tried to get my husband into rehabilitation.

When I assertively asked for marriage counseling, he tried to get what he wanted by saying something that made me feel guilty, like if I had a job, he would not feel so stressed out and need a drink. When words no longer worked, he would try to control me by taking away money for fun kid activities or change his mind about going somewhere. By using intimidation and control tactics, he would try to hurt my feelings or use anger to get his way. My husband used aggressive communication when I was assertive, attempting to manipulate me.

Now it is easier for me to spot people manipulating the situation to get what they want.

Many people would say that by being assertive you bring on your own troubles. You are constantly a target for nastiness. Why be assertive if it is only going to cause you more grief? I can see how many times that I shifted to someone who uses the passive communication style when my husband became aggressive. Passive communication is based on compliance in hopes to avoid confrontation at all costs. Passive people have learned that it is safer not to react, and it is better to disappear than to stand up for oneself and get noticed. I could see when my husband wanted me to be one of those passive people. Yes, the goal is to move to safer waters and let God do the heavy lifting. But what if you cannot physically move? What if you cannot leave the situation?

Do you use assertive communication knowing your household is going to become aggressive?

Communication is never clear-cut.

In bad situations, people who cannot get away from each other physically resort to the last type of communication style:

passive-aggressive. This approach avoids direct confrontation (passive) but attempts to get even through manipulation (aggressive). This devious and sneaky style keeps the fight just below the surface. It never really solves anything, just keeps the status quo. (Styles of Communication, n.d. angelfire.com)[13] When I look back, I can see how many times my husband and I would both use a passive-aggressive approach to get our way. We both would never say exactly what we would mean, and for me it was out of self-preservation. I did not want to get hurt, nor did I want the kids around anger. I assume for my husband it was a way of controlling the situation.

So how does someone become a patient warrior using proper communication with all this anger and manipulation going on every day? A good start is to start by exercising assertive communication according to steps outlined in scripture. The passage below describes the steps very clearly:

> If your brother sins against you, go and tell him his fault, between you and him alone. If he listens to you, you have gained your brother. But if he does not listen, take one or two others along with you, that every charge may be established by the evidence of two or three witnesses. If he refuses to listen to them, tell it to the church. And if he refuses to listen even to the church, let him be to you as a Gentile and a tax collector. (Mt 18:15–17 ESV)[14]

God wants us to speak up when those around us are having bad behavior. However, most people choose passive communication coupled with prayer because it is safer. Their excuses for not speaking up range from not wanting to hurt the feelings of people in pain to nothing will change if they do speak up. Unfortunately, what passive people do not understand is that we are all one body in Christ, and as Christians, we are called to help. This is clearly indicated by the following passage:[15]

Each of you must put off falsehood and speak truthfully, for we are all members of one body. (Eph 4:25 NIV)

The patient warrior needs to get in the mind frame that God cannot use us as an instrument for change if we are silent. As the arms and legs of the body of Christ, we are the "doers." God knows that we are limited in what we can achieve, so he also gives us a plan to follow. That way we know when to stop beating our heads against a stonewalled soul bent to remain unchanged.

God's plan is simple enough on paper. First, honestly and quietly, tell the offender there is a problem using assertive communication. If there is no change, then gather two or three close friends or relatives and try again. If there is no result, then seek help from the church. If the church speaks, and there still no change, you have done your part. This is easier said than done. Many times, each attempt at truthful communication is met with aggressive combatant anger from the other side or worse, passive-aggressive manipulation.

Our challenge as a patient warrior is to not use aggressive communication in return or revert to passive-aggressive tactics out of retaliation. The goal should be to control one's temper with the knowledge that in the end, God knows the truth.

When we receive aggressive behavior in return is when we need to remember how God works. Instead of being the warrior who takes the city, it is better to patiently wait, speaking the truth when called upon to do so and letting God work through your actions. As we speak the truth, we grow our relationship with Christ because telling the truth to someone who does not want to hear it takes guts and perseverance. Guts and perseverance take prayer and thus a stronger relationship with God. This is indicated by the following:[16]

As we lovingly speak the truth, we will grow up completely in our relationship to Christ. (Eph 4:15 GWT)

For me, being a patient warrior is difficult when to the outside world you appear to have the perfect family. It allows the manipulation that is occurring to continue unchecked by others. In addition, finding the few people to help you is difficult enough, but when you appear to have everything neatly arranged, it is impossible. When looking back at my attempts at being a patient warrior, I noticed this vital flaw. We had two kids, a dog, dad with a good job, and mom working part-time and volunteering for the church. In addition, the house was almost paid off, there was no debt, and retirement funds were plentiful. We had dinner every night at a table together. We took vacations to see each side of the family tree every year, plus a vacation to Disney World. We appeared to be the perfect, happy family. I kept everything in motion to make sure we had the perfect, happy family despite what was happening under the surface. Inside the house, turmoil was brewing.

Having tried assertive communication and trying to get his mother to discuss treatment options, I knew that it was time for the next step in God's communication plan. Unfortunately, my husband refused to go to marriage counseling with the priests. No matter how I phrased it, he just would not hear of sitting down with anyone to discuss our issues. The abuse was worsening, and there were times I would say to myself, *God has a plan.* I was patient, and I was a warrior. I kept trying to work the communication plan prescribed in the Bible.

When my ability to become the perfect patient warrior was failing, I should have realized that God would step in. My life could not have looked bleaker. I could not find a full-time job so I could leave with my kids, and I could not get help from people around me. I could not even get to speak to priests with my husband in tow. What was I to do? My husband was off running his own errands most weekends, drinking while he drove around.

But God had a plan.

One Saturday, I held a meeting to prepare materials for the upcoming religious education year. Everyone enjoyed volunteering for my events because they were well organized and full of purpose, so I was told. Over a hundred families came to sort and file lessons into a yearly plan. We prepared crafts to go with each lesson, packing each week's materials in a box, stacking as we went. I had arranged stations for everyone, and each family worked together getting tasks for the year completed.

It was interesting to see God try to work. I had brought the kids with me; I knew my husband would off "running his errands." Everything was perfect until my husband showed up. I saw my husband having a conversation with our priest outside the building we were working in. I thought that it was odd; the physical stance of the priest and my husband was "off" somehow, but I was too busy directing my event to get involved. My husband left shortly after without coming in to say hello. At that moment, my husband finally received counseling from a priest. Later that evening, I found out that the conversation was at the request of a church member and was about being drunk on the property. My husband blamed me for the priest knowing about his condition, which caused a tirade that evening.

It was at that time that the abuse started to move to an everyday occurrence. Life became much worse as time wore on.

Just what do you do when you have followed the biblically prescribed method of dealing with someone who is unchristian, and you are worse off than when you started? At this point the Bible says you are done; leave it to God to fix. However, it is not over, not when it is a family member that you are living with. What do you do? Pray? Leave? Barricade the door?

CHAPTER 8

Finding Out How to Feel Again and Confusing Happiness with Joy

Happiness and fun are good, but they come and go with circumstances. Joy, however, is felt beyond our circumstances. Joy can be experiences even when times are difficult. As we view the events of our lives, we can choose to be resentful toward God for letting things happen to us, or we can choose an attitude of gratitude and a commitment to joy. When we hurry in life, we have the tendency to have a deep anger because we have relinquished the peace that comes from spending times with ourselves and the Lord. When personal growth comes to a halt, it is because our spirit has not had times of stillness.[17]
—Emilie Barnes

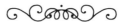

What the kids remember from this time is their parents were together, and they had a happy life. They don't remember going grocery shopping or playing outside because their dad was in a bad mood. They just don't remember how much effort I put in so they never saw their dad in a negative light. All the pictures of the kids' early life had my husband and the kids together, happy. No one seems to remember who took the pictures, though. No matter how hard I tried not to leave their dad so the kids would not come from a broken home, the result was still the same. The kids lost their happy life. What is worse, the kids remember the happiness, never seeing the bad. They cannot fathom why "I had to make Dad leave." I kept the marriage going for them, and when I couldn't anymore, my kids couldn't see the flaws that were there all along. In their eyes, I was the one who made the happy life go away.

When I think about how much energy I put into to keeping up that happy life that was not real, I am amazed. I begged everyone to help me determine what was wrong with my husband medically. When I found out it was alcoholism, I begged everyone to help me help him. I begged God to heal him. When no help came from either, I became very resentful of both the people around me and of God. After all, I did so much for others through the church, wasn't it time for me to receive help? Wasn't it my turn?

I resented God for not taking care of me in my time of need and often asked why I was helping so many people but did not receive any help in return. The Christian theme was to take care of others, and they in return will take care of you. However, I felt like the "you watch my back and I'll watch yours" concept had gone mysteriously awry and left me out of the loop. I could see every other family being happy and having fun, but it was like I was looking in from the outside with no way to get around the barriers. I did not feel God's presence during this awful time, and I hated God for abandoning me after I had been so faithful. Life continued to spiral out of control with no hope of me stopping it. Being thankful and full of joy for the gifts God was bestowing on me was an appalling thought. I thought, *How could anyone experience gratitude while going through this pain?* What I did not know was that I had a great deal to be thankful for; the worst was still yet to come.

I was so full of resentment toward everyone for not helping me get my husband to stop drinking that I failed to see no one wanted to sacrifice the joy in their lives to shoulder the pain of mine. They were protecting their lifestyle like a precious gem, and mine was not worth protecting. The happy life that I had created was a fallacy. I needed to start over. I needed to find my way back to being joyful and full of gratitude.

There was no joy in living at the point where I was because I was just going from one day to the next, trying to keep all the balls in the air. Happiness hinged on my husband's mood and antics. I needed to be reminded that I had gotten away from God's plans for me.

The drinking and verbal abuse was so bad that I began to take weekend trips without my husband. The children and I went to Gatlinburg, Tennessee, with my parents for a week; it was the first time we had traveled without him. I had not experienced that type of peace since before the marriage. I silently prayed he would have drunk himself into oblivion by the time we returned home, and we would never have to experience his antics again. However, my prayers were in vain.

When we returned nothing had changed. My husband drank profusely every day after work, and all day on the weekends. He drove around doing errands and drank; he drank on his way home from work. I prayed he would receive a DUI; however, one never came. While at a church fundraiser, he drank so much that many people came to me telling me was drinking, which I knew already from the wine stains that were down his shirt. I just asked simply, "What do you want me to do? There is nothing that I can do to stop him. Stop serving him drinks."

At Easter, I saw a glimmer of hope. That Easter was the first time my husband listened to me about not traveling to his parent's house. I was still very upset about the stories my father-in-law was telling, and we stayed home for first time. My mother-in-law was quite shocked and called to apologize about the events surrounding Thanksgiving. She stated she was glad she had someone who cared enough to pester her son about his drinking. The whole fundraiser event and not traveling sparked some recognition in my husband, and he was avidly trying to not drink. However, at that point, I was numb inside and at the point of being resentful.

I remember when I first went to my priest and told him about my husband's alcoholism. He asked, "How do you feel?" I went blank; I stared, and I said, "I don't know what you mean." He just asked again, "How do you feel?" I truly had no answer; I had not "felt" for a long time. Yes, I was emotional, I was vocal, but I was numb inside. It was not until then that I realized that I had nothing inside me anymore. No passion for life, no goals. I was just moving from day to day trying to keep everything in motion. I had many balls to keep in the air. I could keep everything in motion. Not just the laundry, meals, and correspondence, but life. It never mattered if it was with family life, volunteer work, or work life, people always knew that I would get the job done, whatever the job, whatever it took. For so many years, I have heard "she" can handle it. "She" will have it organized, and "she" does not need us; we do not need to worry. Not that I made the decisions, I didn't. However, when they decided, I created and executed the plan.

In retrospect, this work ethic caused havoc with my marriage. I thought since my husband worked and I stayed home, we were supposed to be a team. I was doing my part. Unfortunately, what I did not realize until years later is that by keeping everything in motion, I was enabling him to treat me poorly. I was the receiver of tasks that he did not want to do himself. In addition, while I was hurrying around in my life keeping all the balls in the air for everyone, I became very angry and resentful that people were not helping out. Not only was I not spending quality time with others having fun, but I was also not spending any time alone with God.

While I was helping everyone else, I felt that I had many good friends. But for at least five years, when my husband's drinking was at its worst, everyone knew of his alcoholic ways but me. However, not one person stopped him from driving drunk with my children. Not one person asked me how I was doing. I found out the hard way that the people who I thought were my friends were not just fair-weather friends; they were not even interested in my life.

My biggest resentment is that I went through most of the devastating debilitating early years of my marriage alone, without family or friends to help me or to console me, or even to look out for my children. Help never came in the early years. For a long time, I even felt this same way about God. I felt like I was his servant, but not something loved. I had been a diligent volunteer. Although I was working for church projects, I was unfortunately not really spending quality time with God.

My job in God's eyes was to keep trying to make it work out, so I thought. In this scenario, I had to be strong and organized and set boundaries for consequences. Thus, I had tried to stay and fix the marriage. I even started a massive job search so I could get out of the marriage. However, the jobs never came, the drinking never stopped, and the abuse never ended. I had to come to realize that God works in a way that I do not understand.

It wasn't until I stopped keeping all the balls from falling that I realized that God was waiting for me to get out of the way so he could get to work. I was angry because I thought that God was doing nothing but watching, but I failed to recognize that my ability to solve problems was hampering God's progress. God was giving consequences to people around me. However, I never let them feel God's pain so they could grow. Their growth would have helped me. However, I was so busy thinking I was a good volunteer for God; I did not realize how God was trying to work.

In addition, I took no time for myself, so I had also stopped learning, personally, professionally, and spiritually. I had truly relinquished the peace that comes from spending time with myself and the Lord. Even when I was physically still, my mind was always thinking and planning for the next event. My personal growth had come to a halt, and my spirit had not been allowed a time of stillness for quite a while. When I had down time, I never exercised my mind, but merely daydreamed of a fantasy life I could never obtain. My spiritual and personal growth had stopped a decade before. I just did not realize it until I looked at my life in reverse. When I started to analyze what choices led me to where I was, I started to realize how I was undoing God's plan.

I should have looked at my life backward sooner. I maybe could have seen that I was so busy with tasks that I was not centering a piece of my life on God. Maybe the angry parts of my life, the parts that were not going my way, would have been different if I had stopped undoing God's work.

It must take a great deal of effort to get all of us humans moving in alignment to make one event happen. Part of God's plan is consequences that result in learning; however, if we problem solvers come through and take over, God has to start all over. We problem solvers, although useful to God, can also be detrimental to God's overall plan. A better use of our time might be to step back and pray. Try to ask God what he wants us to do instead of jumping in when there is a problem. Maybe the problem is there for a reason, and we are not supposed to fix it.

So here we are again, with the big question. When the biblically prescribed method of dealing with conflict is not working, does that mean that prayer for deliverance is all that is left?

CHAPTER 9

The Canaanite Woman of the Twenty-First Century

Leaving that place, Jesus withdrew to the region of Tyre and Sidon. A Canaanite woman from that vicinity came to Him, crying out, "Lord, Son of David, have mercy on me! My daughter is suffering terribly from demon-possession."

Jesus did not answer a word. So his disciples came to Him and urged Him, "Send her away, for she keeps crying out after us." He answered, "I was only sent to the lost sheep of Israel."

The woman came and knelt before Him. "Lord, help me!" she said. He replied, "It is not right to take the children's bread and toss it to their dogs." "Yes, Lord," she said, "but even the dogs eat the crumbs that fall from their master's table."

Then Jesus answered, "Woman, you have great faith! Your request is granted." And her daughter was healed from that very hour. (Mt 15:21–28) [18]

As mothers, we want our children to have the best. As Americans, we view it as our right to have the best. However, many times our finances do not allow each child to have what others do. That does not stop mothers from trying, though. Mothers are a special breed. They become selfless entities that provide everything to their young. Mothers will go to any length possible to ensure their children are well taken care of, that they are fed, clothed, taught, and above all else, protected from harm. Mothers are vigilant, ever on the watch for danger. When life becomes muddled from stress, mothers become vigilantes of justice, searching out the wrongdoers of their offspring.

Just watch any group of young mothers supervising their children on a playground. The mothers, whether they know each other or not, begin to discuss a variety of topics from home remedies to toy purchases. Next, they move on to choices of schools to behavioral issues. As they depart each mother internally compares her situation with her counterparts to determine equality. They ask themselves *What am I not providing for my kids? How do I provide what she is providing?*

I think this is where the need to be a task juggler comes in. When we as mothers do not feel that we are fulfilling our duty of providing for all the wants and needs of our children, we squeeze in one more errand or child activity. After all, it is for the sake of providing the best for our offspring. Young mothers fall into a trap of "provide or the child will get left behind."

But when surrounded by the continual upheaval of normalcy, mothers can become vigilantes for justice. Mothers can require justice for wrongdoings on the playground as well as mean looks from across the room. The same group of women who were sharing recipes can be at the same playground a week later running around demanding toys be returned, sand not thrown, or apologies made. When surrounded by chaos, a mother's go-to position is protecting the children from everything.

There was upheaval of normalcy in my house all right. I had also become a vigilante mama. It didn't matter what kids offended my kids; I wanted it stopped. I wanted my children to have the perfect life. What I did not put together was that the lack of normalcy at home was affecting every aspect of our lives. I was afraid of the other shoe dropping constantly. This made me emotional at the drop of a hat. I felt if I kept giving to my kids, they would somehow feel like all of the kids around them.

To provide more opportunities for my children, I juggled more balls in the air as the years wore on. I volunteered for more kid-friendly functions at the church. I volunteered at clothing and toy exchanges at churches so I could provide better clothes and an abundance of toys. Many people asked me to do many things. However, in looking back on my life, I said yes to a many projects that maybe were not of God's asking. By the time the kids were both potty trained, they knew where all the bathrooms were in three different church buildings of our parish. By the time they were both in school, I was on committees of three different parishes. I rationalized that this was how I socialized with the women around me. I didn't go shopping or out for coffee; I volunteered. What I did not recognize was that these tasks were a way for me to avoid dealing with the problems in my life.

Here I was, working at every church function that was asked of me and praying God would heal my husband as well as my marriage for the sake of my children. I begged God to point out the path and bring us back to a sound, happy family; my children were suffering. However, I was met with silence. I rationalized to God that I was equally as good as all the other mothers, so why could my children not have the advantages that their children have? Still silence. I was faithful in my pursuit of God and his answers, but my begging turned to yelling for his attention. Still silence. I needed to get out of the terrible situation I had gotten into. I never felt so betrayed. Betrayed by my husband, yes, but also by everyone in that church who was supposed to watch out for me as good Christians should. I was teaching their youth in one building while they were watching my husband usher drunk in the church the next building over. For five years, no one said anything to me, close friends and priests included. I was devastated that no one came to my aid, but moreover, I felt discarded by God. I had become a church doormat. I had become the person you can go to in order get stuff done, knowing they would not turn you down. I was a part of the church, but not a crucial part. I was like the vacuum cleaner, stored in a closet until needed then used to clean up messes created at parties—only to be stored again without much thought. When the party is going on, no one thinks about the vacuum cleaner.

One Sunday, I went to church alone for daily mass, just by chance. I was ready to walk away from God, being distraught and dejected by his silence. It was then I heard a young priest's interpretation of the story of the Canaanite woman, and that interpretation hit home with me. A young priest, whom I had never heard speak before, said God used the Canaanite woman to teach those who were standing around watching the story unfold about the true meaning of faith and perseverance. Throughout his homily, I began to identify with his interpretation, as many were watching my story unfold as well. I wanted to hear the rest of the lesson. As I sat there, I began to weep uncontrollably, so much so that I wanted to leave, but could not. A parishioner I did not know came over to sit by me just to comfort me.

To summarize the young priest's lesson for the day, God was using the Canaanite woman's grief as a way of getting the attention of those around her. She never faltered in her pursuit of God; she continually spoke up for the healing of her child. Even when she was denigrated by those around her, she still sought assistance from God. When she was met with God's rebuff, she continued, knowing His power was all that was needed to set life back on a correct course. All these conversations with God took place while people around her watched, quietly doing nothing. It was not the Canaanite woman herself that was being taught a lesson on how to be truly faithful to God. It was those around her. The Canaanite woman knew God's power and that it was all that was needed to cure her and her child's immense suffering. Someone in the crowd of spectators was being shown the true meaning of faith and perseverance.

While listening to the priest's lesson, I asked God, "Why couldn't the spectators be given the terrible consequences to deal with so they could learn faith and perseverance firsthand?" Almost as if on cue, the priest went into a deeper level of interpretation. He answered my question to God eloquently by stating, "If God put the lookers-on in situations that were as detrimental as what the Canaanite woman was going through, they would turn and run from God, like the chafe blowing away from the wheat." The spectators' faith was not strongly developed; they need to witness what true faith in God was so they themselves can be drawn on that knowledge later when the time to test their faith was upon them.

As I sat in church weeping, I wanted to know who around me was weak in faith, who was it who was allowed to watch my suffering. Why wasn't this person not learning their vital lesson? When would the suffering of my children end and their childhood begin? How much more pain would I and my children have to bear for the sake of Christians who were only coming to Christ as a fad to be one of the crowd? I did not feel like a blessed soul. I felt like we were being put on display, with this message: *"The pain and suffering you can receive from God is real. Pay attention."*

As time marched on in our lives, I tried to believe that the suffering would end. I still begged God for relief of my husband's alcoholism and abuse. However, nothing came. Had I missed God's lesson? God can make any situation be a lesson for good. God can make anything happen. Why was God waiting?

THE
STANDOFF

CHAPTER 10

What Are the Options?

Along the way you will stumble, and perhaps even
fall; but that, too, is normal and to be expected. Get
up, back on your feet, chastened but wiser.
—Anonymous

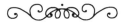

Let's take stock of the situation. After years of infertility
treatments, I had two children, both born after high-risk pregnancies.
During a church service after the birth of my first child, my daughter,
I heard a song about God crying out for someone to help his people
find him. I asked to God "send me" because he had given me all that
I have ever wanted. My son, our second child, was born early due to
his kidney complications and my husband's alcoholism.

The dream life that I thought God had given me turned out to be
a nightmare. My children were growing up in chaos, despite my best
efforts as a stay-at-home mom. Although my children attended a strict
Catholic school, many of the families there were not sympathetic to
our home life with an alcoholic. The school was extremely small, with
one class per grade. There was no doubt that everyone knew everyone
else's business. Regardless, in the end, no one helped to protect my
children from their alcoholic father.

Years later I was sitting in a pew, in the same church where I asked

God to "send me," and I was listening to a homily on the Canaanite woman. I was crying my eyes out and feeling abandoned by God. I was devastated from handling an alcoholic husband alone. I saw or heard very little from my family or my in-laws. One by one the couples at our wedding drifted away. The friends I volunteered with continued to ask for my abilities to whip events into shape, but they steered clear of any involvement in my personal life.

I had yet to realize that I had stumbling blocks that were holding me back from what I needed to do. I had been too busy combating life to take the time to learn from the situation I was in. The list of stumbling blocks that I had yet to figure out that I had are below:

1. Blindness. I had yet to learn that even people you love can be dishonest. But more importantly, I turned a blind eye and did not ask myself the tough questions when situations seemed off. I taught myself to be ignorant.

2. No boundaries. I was too capable for my own good, which led to having no boundaries. Since I did not set boundaries from the beginning, there was no hope of creating them after time went on.

3. Anger. Anger at myself for being irresponsible when things did not go my way. Anger at my husband for being so mean. Anger at my family for not helping. Angry at my husband's family for continuing to ignore the problem and anger at the people around me from the church and school for not getting involved.

4. No self-esteem. Surrendering my own opinion. "Pride goes before the fall," but I thought I was never right. I had no beliefs of my own, and it did not matter what the topic was. Not having an ability to examine my thoughts against the thoughts of others was a big stumbling block for me.

5. Impatience. When I began to have the heart-to-heart conversation with God, I was not prepared for a time lag. I was not patient and could not see or hear God's answer.

6. My strength. It took examining my soul with God to find out that my worldly strength was my stumbling block.

Unfortunately, I did not realize I had these stumbling blocks until after soul-searching conversations with God. My conversations here on earth were as varied as the stars. There were quiet ones as well as loud ones. I had these conversations wherever I went, but mostly I sat in the pews at the three churches I volunteered at. As I sat crying in my pew, I felt like God was leaving me on my own to figure out this situation. I started asking myself what type of options I had. As I sobbed, I thought about all kinds of options, job options, where my children and I could live, and how leaving or staying would play out with my husband.

Each trip home from church was the same. I would look at my circumstance from all sides. We were upper middle class. Was my situation unheard of? My husband went to work at a great job every day; he never missed work. He was not an angry and violent man away from home, and everyone thought he was great. But when we walked into the door at home, we were afraid of the man who stepped out of his skin. There was no provocation, just a lightning-fast difference. I just couldn't attribute the violence to a cause anymore. There was no cause that I knew of, other than in my husband's eyes I could not do anything right. I knew we needed help, and I knew I needed to come up with a plan.

So why didn't I just leave? Many people ask this very question of women in violent situations. It would make sense to just get up and leave. But the decision to leave an abusive relationship is not as straightforward as it might seem. Yes, domestic violence assaults are repeated against the same victim by the same person. But domestic violence is more about a series of repeated nonviolent behaviors that are designed to control the spouse rather than one or two physical events.

It's the verbal abuse breaking down self-esteem or the financial abuse that keeps victims tied to their abuser. Many times, there is sexual abuse that is designed to make victims feel ashamed. While the physical assaults might occur infrequently, the other parts of the abuse pattern occur daily. This daily subliminal abuse causes a profound effect on the victims. Victims are made to feel like they deserve everything the spouse dishes out.

So what were my options?

If I left without the kids, I would have nothing—no children, no place to live, nothing. The kids would be left alone with their father, who drank profusely. I knew other women who tried this route. Their idea was they would fight for their kids when they were more established. But I bet their kids felt abandoned, growing up in fear and feeling worthless with no hope. When I looked at women I knew who made this choice, their children grew up in unstable settings. The children had no one to fight for them directly. They could not see progress. To make matters worse, the dads were either not present, passed out, or drunk beyond control. In this situation, the kids began numbing themselves from the situation with their own budding addictions. Every kid I knew grew into a mini version of their addicted dad. Eventually, the moms used the kids' drinking and drug abuse in the courts, but the damage had already been done.

This was not going to be my plan of choice.

I thought about moving into the shelter with the children and fighting my husband from that vantage point. But if I took the children into a shelter, they would be afraid of their surroundings. Eventually there would be a fight for custody, and I would lose because I did not have a permanent place to live. Then there were the sleeping arrangements—an open room with beds lined up against the wall. The lack of privacy would not be ideal, and I would be forever on the alert for theft. These thoughts paled in comparison to the thoughts of my kids being violated physically.

No, a shelter was not an option.

To be honest, it was safer for the children if we all stayed put, living with the alcoholic. Quite simply, if I was still in the home, I could monitor my husband's interactions with the children. While

I fought to keep everyone safe, I would keep looking for a full-time job.

One thing that I learned during this time was not to compare myself with others. What was right for other women was not right for me. Those who left their children may have had good reasons that I could not see. And those that entered shelters may have had better shelters to go to. Everyone's life has different options. Each of us must take responsibility for doing the best we can with the options given to us. We must also realize that we are a part of the overall plan God is working out for everyone. What we are going through and how we choose to react effect parts of God's master plan.

CHAPTER 11

Souls Are Saved by the Truth and Betrayed by the Spread of Lies
(Prv 14:25)[19]

Lying is just another form of running. It's using manipulation to get out of a tough situation instead of relying on God to work things out.[20]
—Pete Wilson

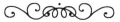

Remember, my husband's behavior changes didn't occur every day. It wasn't like I married Dr. Jekyll and knew Mr. Hyde was waiting for me when I got home. When it started, it was every once and a while. He said or did something that was "off," and I just couldn't put my finger on what it was. Over time, the frequency of those events became closer together. Then the "offness" turned to a blatant disregard for my personal well-being. Armed with a sense of purpose, I searched online and in local bookstores for a meaningful way to rectify my situation. I openly read books on alcoholism and codependency.

Much of the information I was looking for were options to turn my husband's behavior back around. I wanted him back to the man I married. But I did not find any recipe for fairy dust that would change him back to the man that he used to be. There was only one solution that I could find in all the literature—and that was to leave.

Over time, I began to look for something else in my literature review, that magic moment when we label someone we love as an abuser and ourselves as the victim. I know it sounds strange, but just when is it? The first time they yell and scream at you for an hour, or do they need to hit you? Or is it after some sort of pattern is established? Just when do you label poor behavior as abuse *before* you are raped or murdered? I never found the answer to any of these questions.

However, during my readings, I found this interesting quote, and I slowly began to realize that I was *allowing* myself to be a victim:[21]

> Domestic violence is not a matter of class, race or socioeconomic status. It is a gender issue. Most batterers are male; however, most men are not batterers. Batterers often share the following characteristics: uses intimidation, is verbally abusive, minimizes abuse, has substance abuse issues, breaks or strikes things in anger, projects blame, is cruel to animals or children, has controlling behavior, isolates themselves and their victims, has Dr. Jekyll and Mr. Hyde behavior between public and private lives, spiritually and religiously abuses their victims, and uses privilege as a form of control.
> —National Domestic Violence Hotline

This was a strange time. Lies were everywhere. I was dealing with habitual lying of an adult. I had never been in this situation before. My husband's lies had become a part of our family's communication structure. He would lie about how much he had to drink and how much he had spent. So naturally, I added books on lying to my repertoire.

I often wondered if there was ever a right time to tell a lie. We lie to protect feelings, to keep secrets, to be liked, and to manipulate others into giving us control.

This passage from Matthew gives us the best perspective on whether lying is acceptable.

> What comes out of the mouth proceeds from the heart, and this can defile a person. For out of the heart can come evil thoughts, murder, adultery, sexual immorality, theft, false witness, slander. (Mt 15:18–20)[22]

Put more plainly, when someone lies, it is a window to what is in their heart. So that is where we need to start the examination of a lie, by looking at what is in the heart. Once the true reason for the lie is determined, we then need to continue the examination by looking at whether the lie is hurting more than it is helping. The passage from Matthew warrants a closer look.

When we examine lying, we can see that lies are a form of protection for the liar. But protection from what? From pain, whether it be physical or emotional. That manipulative lying is tied in with self-esteem; as soon as people feel that their self-esteem is threatened, they immediately begin to tell bigger lies, according to Robert Feldman. When my husband lied, he was trying to cover up a deep emotional shortcoming. But when he reached the stage where he would use Bible passages to justify his lying and actions, I knew that I could no longer be a patient warrior waiting for God to intervene. I had to leave no matter the cost. I think we all have had people twist half of a verse so it suits them. For my husband it was Ephesians 5: 21–33.[23] Or as we called it in our house, *"Wives, obey your husbands!"*

Here's a refresher on the complete version of Ephesians 5: 21–33:

> Out of respect for Christ, be courteously reverent to one another. Wives, understand and support your husbands in ways that show your support for Christ. The husband provides leadership to his wife the way Christ does to his church, not by domineering but by

cherishing. So just as the church submits to Christ as he exercises such leadership, wives should likewise submit to their husbands. Husbands, go all out in your love for your wives, exactly as Christ did for the church—a love marked by giving, not getting. Christ's love makes the church whole. His words evoke her beauty. Everything he does and says is designed to bring the best out of her, dressing her in dazzling white silk, radiant with holiness. And that is how husbands ought to love their wives. They're really doing themselves a favor—since they're already "one" in marriage. No one abuses his own body, does he? No, he feeds and pampers it. That's how Christ treats us, the church, since we are part of his body. And this is why a man leaves father and mother and cherishes his wife. No longer two, they become "one flesh." This is a huge mystery, and I don't pretend to understand it all. What is clearest to me is the way Christ treats the church. And this provides a good picture of how each husband is to treat his wife, loving himself in loving her, and how each wife is to honor her husband. (Eph 5: 21–33)

Here is what my husband took from this long Bible lesson:

Wives, support your husbands. The husband provides leadership to his wife the way Christ does to his church. So, just as the church submits to Christ as he exercises leadership, wives should likewise submit to their husbands.

Yes, this was selective hearing (or reading) at its best. It would have been comical had it not been for the irrational abuse attached to it.

So, there I sat with all my books, knowing I needed to leave but not having a job to support me. However, it seems like no matter where I turned or who I asked, the doors and windows were locked, with no hope of opening. Sometimes events need to shift to pull you out of a situation you are in. I prayed for a shift in circumstance, I begged, and I became disillusioned.

CHAPTER 12

Mad That You Are Missing the Point—
So Let Me Tell You About It Again

God loves you enough to strip away anything
that gets between his relationship with you. God
made his purpose clear. He is not interested in our
having a good life. He is interested in an intimate
relationship with us. He is interested in our spiritual
transformation. It is in the middle of crisis that we
are ready to listen to Him.[24]
—Pete Wilson

How many times do we pray for something—over and over? I
prayed for my husband to get better. I prayed for a job so I could
afford to leave him. I prayed for the safety of my children. I prayed
for help from other people. And I didn't pray all the same way. My
prayers were prayers of all kinds. They were soft. They were tearful.
My prayers were in a group of people. My prayers were in solitude and
meditative. And when that did not work, I prayed by screaming at the
top of my lungs.

I was pouring out my miseries. My message was clear. My heart
was breaking for a life I longed to have. But remember, God works
differently. God hears melodies in honest cries for help. Not that he

takes pleasure in our pain, but he knows that the only time we will be ready to hear him is when we are in a crisis. I was crashing into my stumbling blocks, and to God, this was better than an alleluia. God was ready to give me the answer to my prayers in a clear message.

God's answer to everything was "no." My only solution, I thought, was to continue by taking back that baton of "doer, helper, and oh-most-capable-one."

Life started to hit the fan when I began to question our finances. Our budget and financial planning was simplistic. We had one joint credit card, and we each had a joint checking account that we were responsible for, although we were not allowed to write checks on each other's. We put all items except for major purchases on the credit card and paid it off at the end of the month. My husband's goal was to not have a credit card bill of over $1,000 per month, which I commended.

My husband would get belligerent any time there were questions about our finances. In addition, he spread the bills out by date on the kitchen table and would go berserk if they were touched. I did not have a problem flying blind, so to speak. What was difficult was trying to feed a family of four and having gas money for transportation to school fifteen miles away on $1,000 a month. I knew from his tirades about the bills not to ask for more money, so I supplemented the $1,000 with money from my part-time teaching jobs. These little positions made $1,000 manageable, but my husband then limited his already meager stipend of funds to $600, and it was tough. But the part-time teaching jobs allowed me to cover what was needed when the $600 did not last the month. As time progressed, my husband felt the need to cut up the credit card, even though it did not have a balance, and provide his stipend in grocery cards. He also reduced the stipend to $400 a month. He started demanding that I go to the priest for money to pay for the kids' Catholic school tuition, stating that I volunteered so much I should be a paid employee. When I asked to be involved in paying the bills and preparing of the taxes, his tirade broke loose. I told him I just could not believe that we were in that dire of a situation.

The verbal abuse was debilitating. The kids started to have problems in school with their grades. After begging my husband to get help and speaking to the school about the kids' problems, a teacher recommended that we go to therapy. She mentioned that the school counselor was free while school was in session and our insurance would probably cover the cost of a therapist when school let out. I asked my husband to agree to put the kids in therapy, but he said no. However, we started anyway with the school counselor, and when school was out, we moved to someone that our insurance would cover, excluding the copayment. I thanked that teacher; I was so depressed and alone I had never thought of the insurance company.

I also went to the family crisis center for advice. The counselor there said I needed to start documenting the events surrounding the drinking and verbal abuse. Therapy would be a way to help document our problems as well. I found a family therapist through a friend. She had taken her daughter to someone who she thought was practical. When I contacted her and explained the situation about the abuse and refusal from my husband to allow us to seek counseling, she agreed to see us each privately. The counselor saw us four times each, all separately, prior to asking us to invite my husband to the sessions. The kids and I did not tell my husband about going; we were afraid of what would happen.

It was about that time when my part-time teaching jobs were becoming infrequent due to the lack of students, leaving me with about $1,000 in my checking account. I was using this money to pay for the copays to the counselor. When we began to see the family therapist, she said to do nothing for my husband, not even have sex. She said that he needed to learn to fend for himself until he learned to treat us better. It was then that my husband had a tirade about not having sex. His statement was, "You will have sex with me, make it really good, and make me think that you want it, or I will take all the money out of your checking account." I was more concerned with my children's mental health than my distaste for him, so I played my part. The next day, I moved my money to an individual account. I also wrote a letter to the therapist to serve as a reminder to him when he started going to therapy.

My husband was becoming physically abusive in front of kids. A battle of wills between my husband and our now seven-year-old son began, starting with our son being pinned down by the wrists one night and his dad yelling at him within inches of his face. "Do you like going to your school? If you don't listen to me, I will put you in the cheapest school there is." When I told my husband he had made his point, he responded by saying he was not trying to make a point to our son; he was trying to make a point to me. Our son said later that he forgave his dad, but forgiving is different from loving.

Later that week my husband tried to take our daughter to run errands. He was inebriated; he could not get his car to start, nor could he get the key out of ignition. He left her in the car as he searched the house for another set of keys. He violently refused to let me take her out of the car. He finally just took my car. Fortunately, he forgot about our daughter altogether as she was in his car. I retrieved her after her dad left. When he returned, he passed out with her in her bed after asking her to go to AA meetings with him. She was ten years old. That evening a mechanic came. He said the problem was that my husband put the car in drive before he turned the key in the ignition. He had left our daughter strapped in a car that was in drive while he was searching for other keys, too belligerent to allow me to remove her while he was searching.

When the therapist said it was time to have him come in, my husband went but was not happy about it. He did go, though; all of us had individual appointments. By my husband's fourth appointment, he had the therapist convinced I was the cause of his drinking. Without someone right there to counteract his lying, it was just a he-said-she-said game. The kids really didn't want to say anything about anything because they loved us both. They didn't want to tattle, and I did not force them to.

Life at home was unbearable from the time my husband came home until he passed out. The weekends were especially dangerous when he came home drunk from drinking and driving as he ran errands. I began to call the police for safety reasons. However, because I had no visible bruises, the best that they could do was inform me he could be taken to jail or to his brother's house.

Until I could document the physical abusive with pictures, I was still trapped. My husband rarely left large bruises. He shoved me around by body checking me. He straddled me to hold me down. He threw things at me. But as for using his hands for punching and strangling, that was yet to come. The children threw up almost every day from the stress of living in this terrible environment. I continued to write our family priest about my feelings. However, his reply was still the same—only the Holy Spirit from within ourselves can truly guide us.

I continued to pray—loudly. I was suffering through this life alone. No parents to give advice, no friends to drive the kids to school. Nothing. Everyone just steered clear. One night, the kids were at a sleepover, and I went to a movie by myself. One of the scenes just clicked with me, and I heard a bit of God's conversation to me. In the scene, a boy was losing a boxing match. His tearful comment to his trainer was, "I am trying to get back up. Why won't you help me?" The trainer's answer was just as emotional. It was "My child, it is because I can no longer see you in pain."

That's when I understood a small portion of my stumbling block issue. I was strong and a fighter. I wanted to drive this problem into the ground. But God knew this was beyond my skill set. I was getting hurt, both physically and emotionally. Unfortunately, God did not give me a glimpse of what I was supposed to be doing. And at this point, I needed a burning bush to come to my door and ring the doorbell.

After the movie, I vowed to take on a lesser role with my husband. We were seeing a counselor. She could take on the role of babysitter for this grown man. However, life is never that easy. The counselor said, "You need to set boundaries and make him deal with his consequences." I thought I had been doing that; I certainly had gotten the reputation that I had not let him get his way. She would say, "Leave things where they lie; he will have to take care of them." I would answer, "His Christmas presents are still where he left them in the living room after he opened them, and it's June, and the refrigerator has been leaking water for a year and a half. That stuff has no effect on him." She would say, "You have all the control; he cannot make a decision without you. You need to leave him, divorce him." I would reply, "I don't have a job, so I cannot afford a lawyer; I have been looking for quite some time. And as far as decisions, he has been deciding what to spend money on and what not to since we were married. He is immediately on the opposite side of anything I suggest. He is in control of everything. If he does not want to do something, he just doesn't."

One rainy night, I received a phone call around dinner time from my husband. He was stranded on the side of the road across from our church. It was getting dark, and the rain was intense. He demanded that I come so he could jump the car with jumper cables. I did not have anyone to watch the children, so I strapped them in and provided them with snacks and drinks for the road. When we arrived, he was livid and sitting on the hood of the car in the pouring rain. I pulled the car in front of his and popped the hood for him. Once he got his car to start and unhooked the two cars, the kids and I proceeded to leave, but the car he was driving would not hold a charge. We had to repeat the whole process. With the thunder and lightning the situation was dangerous. So was the verbal abuse from him. There were threats of beatings if we did not stay.

When the car was running for the second time, the kids and I left. His car moved along fine, so I saw no reason to worry. I wanted to get the kids to their rooms prior to him walking in the door. When we arrived home, the phone was ringing. His car had stopped again, and the verbal abuse was terrifying. I called the family therapist to determine what my course of action should be. She said to leave him on side of road, that he needed to be taught a lesson on the proper way to act. Although I knew it would be a nightmare when he arrived home if I did not return to help him, I did not go. He eventually called a tow truck and had the car dropped off at the mechanic's shop. The tow truck driver dropped him off at the house. Not knowing if he would try to punish me by taking out his anger on the kids, I had all of us, including our dog Lucky, in my bedroom with the door locked. When he arrived, he broke down the bedroom door with his fist as he pushed his way into the bedroom. He screamed at the top of his lungs for what seemed like an eternity. Lucky positioned herself between him and the children, baring her teeth whenever he stepped to close. She was seventy pounds of controlled fury, and eventually my husband went to the basement and passed out on the couch. The rest of us slept together with Lucky and the foot of the bed.

As Thanksgiving approached, my husband became tenser, as did I. One evening was especially dangerous. My father-in-law called to discuss my brother-in-law's thoughts on committing suicide. My husband's entire family lived out of town, except this one brother. He lived about twenty minutes away and was very successful. My father-in-law had a long conversation with my husband concerning the mental health of this successful brother. My husband was genuinely concerned, however, so he drank until he was plastered.

The telephone call spawned several tirades from my husband. He threw cups of coffee. He performed his famous body-blocking moves, shoving me around using his chest while saying "I am not pushing you—I am not using my hands." Next were *his* proclamations that he himself was going to commit suicide. I felt like I was always talking him down off an emotional roller-coaster. His last fit ended with him yelling, "Don't you see, I am trying to get you to divorce me?" and then passing out in bed. After I collected my sanity, I thought it strange that my husband acted this way. It was like the limelight was off him for a moment, and he had to get it back. But why show this emotion to me if he wanted attention from his parents?

I did not want to go to the traditional Thanksgiving event with my husband's relatives. I did not want to repeat a suicide watch. Also, there was more drinking than you can imagine, including underage drinking. When we arrived, my husband drank, even though he allegedly said he went to AA meetings during the weekend. One of my sisters-in-law noticed the demeanor as well. I did my best to ignore or isolate myself from his mayhem. But I brought about three mishaps that set my husband off. I do not have any regrets about it, though.

First, at dinner I had a glass of wine. One glass for a three-day weekend. Knowing that this would upset my daughter if she knew, I said to the twenty-year-old drinking nephew beside me, "If your cousin asks, this is yours!" He said, "OK." Later that evening, the second mishap occurred. My nephew, his seventeen-year-old sister, his mother, and another person were sitting around the fireplace. My nephew was regaling us with his exploits at his campus hotspots. It was a very jovial conversation. I reminded him that I used to help the sheriff's department run prostitution raids in that part of town. I told him that if he saw a Greyhound bus parked on the street with warning triangles around it, that a sting was in operation. I also said that the prostitutes would look just like his sister—normal, wearing jeans and sweatshirts—but they would be standing in one place instead of walking around. The last mishap occurred when the three underaged drinkers (sixteen, seventeen, and twenty) were on the balcony drinking. I went out and politely said, "I just want you to know that your uncle, my husband, started drinking when he was sixteen. He is now an alcoholic. Just be careful and watch yourselves." To me this level of honesty about teenaged drinking was needed. What would be a better example than knowing that an alcoholic you love started drinking at the same age as you were now?

When we arrived home, my husband received a phone call from his brother (the one talking about suicide). Apparently, his children were asking questions about alcoholism, and he was not happy. I never could speak to the brother; all the conversations were filtered through my husband. I was supposed to refute that "I passed my drinking problem off on other people." "I said my niece was sleeping around." "The underage drinkers at Thanksgiving were going turn into alcoholics."

On that evening my husband was especially angry about the situation, he said to me:

> There are three people that you need to talk to. The family therapist [holding up his index finger], the family priest [holding up his middle in addition to his index], and God [putting his index finger down, thus giving God the finger.]

I was quite unnerved at that point. How can a Christian, even an angry one, flip off God? I know how angry I have been at God, but I have never done that.

I called both the counselor and the family priest. My conversation with the priest was filled with weepy tears. I went through everything—the job search, the hidden drinking—and finished by say that I could not handle any of this anymore. Within one hour of speaking to the priest, my husband was drinking and driving. A squirrel jumped out in front of him. He swerved and smashed his car into the curb. He walked to a nearby office building to call me for help finding a tow truck. When I arrived, there were several police around because two different 911 calls had been placed stating they had seen a drunk driver. I told the officers that I thought my husband being arrested was long overdue and praised them profusely. Though our brief conversation, the police realized that my husband had a government clearance and that I did not work. Out of kindness to me, the officer of record reduced the charges from driving under the influence to public intoxication so my husband would not lose his government job. As I was walking away, I could hear my husband scream, "This is all your fault—I never get arrested!" I just left, saying to myself, *You just don't flip off God!*

My husband entered a recovery center within days of the arrest. I was overjoyed. Events had shifted. God had answered as only he could, and I knew that somehow our family would be healed. However, God's plans are never that simple.

Christmas was not that far away, and the holiday became an interesting time; my husband entered on-site rehabilitation, and those first days were helpful. My husband had a rehabilitation counselor who specialized in alcoholics in treatment. This person was gifted. But then my husband was moved to their outpatient program due to insurance reasons. Since life was so difficult with him around, I did not want him living with us while he was addressing his demons. He planned to live with his brother for a week while he looked for an apartment. However, no one wanted to deal with his problem over Christmas, so my husband checked into a hotel. I was not privy to all the details or timing. I know that my parents came on the December 27 for a three-day visit, and before their arrival, they said they did not want to see him.

During this holiday, my husband's goal was to find an apartment. However, within one week of beginning outpatient treatment, the rehabilitation counselor somehow spotted him drinking and got him to admit to drinking in his hotel room. Coincidentally, this happened on December 27. This landed him at the rehabilitation hospital's halfway house. He also had outpatient treatment, what they consider tier two treatment.

On one of his trips from work to the halfway house, my husband left a note for me in the mailbox asking for my parents email address. He thought he had been misrepresented in the whole drinking scenario that landed him in jail and rehabilitation. My parents did not want to have any communication with him ever, and life continued.

CHAPTER 13

Wine Makes You Mean and Beer Makes You Quarrelsome—a Staggering Drunk Is Not Much Fun
(Prv 20:1)[25]

Life with an alcoholic who was always searching for the next drink was not much fun. But what was worse was one who was drinking while trying to hide it from everyone. Sorting out the lies was a full-time job. My husband and I were now seeing the rehabilitation family therapist twice a week. In addition, all four of us were each seeing the family therapist individually once a week. This left me driving the kids to and from school, to and from their events, going to all the counseling sessions for our kids as well as myself, doing all the volunteer functions for the church, and trying to look for full-time work while holding down a part-time sales job—all of this by myself. I was a frazzled mess.

Once, I had a big sales meeting in Chattanooga during the day. During one of our first sessions with the rehabilitation family therapist, I asked my husband if I could trade cars for the day. The car he drove was the one we typically drove daily on the interstate. He said fine. Each visit, I reminded him of the date. The day before the big trip, we had another session with same counselor. After the meeting, as we were walking out, I asked if we were to trade cars then. My husband said, "I don't know." It was 5:00 p.m., and I had kids to pick up at a friend's house, dinner to make, gas to purchase for the trip, etc. I proceeded to my car and left. As I went down the parkway, my husband passed me and then slowed down in front of me. He then proceeded to get off at the next exit. When I went home, I had message on the answering machine from him stating I should have pulled around to where he had parked his car and traded cars. Now the next option for me was to trade in the morning at 7:00 a.m. I had to get up an extra hour and a half early to drive in the opposite direction to trade cars before I left for my meeting.

In our next session with the rehabilitation family therapist, I brought the audio tape from the answering machine for proof of the accounts of that logistic mess. She directly asked my husband, "What made you do that? Don't you see she has to get on with her day?" His answer was, "I don't know."

The rehabilitation family therapist could really get to the heart of the matter. I felt if she could break through to the reason why my husband needed to treat me in such an insane way, we could see our way to the other side of this alcoholic dilemma. However, a huge battle began to evolve between the rehabilitation therapist and the family therapist. The family therapist began to contradict the rehabilitation family therapist's philosophy by saying, "I do not buy into fancy terms like codependency," and "You are the cause your husband's drinking." I would in turn ask the rehabilitation therapist about my role in my husband's drinking, only to hear that I could not make someone drink.

Eventually, he manipulated everything he said at family counseling; there was not one situation that he could not twist to make himself look like the victim. I asked the family therapist to have joint sessions with my husband and me to help eliminate the he-said-she-said game. However, our joint sessions quickly became my husband's time to tell me what to fix about myself while I tried to tackle the budget and payment of weekly grocery and gas bills. During this time, the family therapist quickly clarified her role as "not a mediator." The sessions quickly deteriorated and fueled the cycle of our marital demise downward.

My problems escalated at the family therapist's when my children started to have issues with her. In my opinion, the family therapist was less than compassionate to my daughter during her private sessions. I knew from personal experience with the family therapist you could not ask a question in return to clarify the understanding of question she had just asked. She merely would repeat the same question with increasing condescension. The family therapist's philosophy was that you can tell if a person is honest if when asked a question, they do not need time to think about it. In many of my private sessions I had with the counselor, I would comment on the lack of rapport she had with my daughter by statements like "Our daughter really doesn't like you." "Our daughter hates you." When I confronted the counselor concerning the behavior, she stated, "You don't know what goes on; your daughter is the problem." It was then that I began noticing that my now ten-year-old daughter cried before and after each of her sessions. There was even a time when I forced the kids to go see her because the family counselor said this was part of the healing process. I would bite my lip, saying this is for the best, all the while knowing that she was just as mean to my daughter as she was to me. When I found out one of her techniques of questioning, I was furious. My daughter said the counselor stated, "If you don't have any problems, you must be God—am I talking to God? I don't think you are God, so what are your problems?" This made me angry; I went to the counselor for help. I had never been to a therapist before. I checked her out with a trusted friend. How could I have been so wrong?

The family therapist wanted boundaries set, but I guess telling the truth is not one of them because I when set boundaries, I look controlling and uncompassionate. What's worse, because I tell the truth, I make it look like my husband is the victim. Through all of this, there is the irony that I went to this counselor for help, but it turned out that she was the major factor for influencing my husband to believe he can blame his drinking on me. To make matters worse, my husband had the family therapist convinced that I had him arrested that night he drove into the curb. Somehow, he truly believed that going to jail and being released the next day had occurred because I asked the police to take him.

In sessions with the family therapist, she would say I was the reason my husband drank, and in sessions with the alcohol rehabilitation counselor in the same week, she stated that I had nothing to do with my husband's drinking. Now our dual therapies were dueling with each other.

During this time, the alcohol rehabilitation counselor had recommended I write a letter to my husband to let him see all the terrible hurt he had caused by his drinking. She recommended a laundry list of indiscretions for him to hear once, absolving him of hearing the problems over and over. Her thought was to help him by not adding new hurt on top of old. My husband was supposed to apologize for each offense; the goal was to help the marriage heal.

Since he no longer lived with us, I became better at reading my husband's facial expressions. I had more peaceful time to contemplate and digest the events around me. I thought back and remembered he always had a particular look when he wanted to fill my wine glass, like he was trying to get away with something. I guess he thought it was OK for him to be drinking if I was drinking. While I was writing the laundry list of items for him to apologize for, he burst into the house yelling with that same look on his face. My husband came into the computer area screaming that I was not participating in his therapy because I had not given him the list. I was sitting there with the list almost finished. When I saw the expression in his eyes and on his face, a cold chill ran down my spine. My heart was saying, *Do not give it to him—don't even mention it.* I knew he was trying to get away with something.

I could not believe this process was part of God's plan. I wrote another letter to my priest for some sort of explanation; I needed a sign that everything was going to end up okay. How many lies could be swarming around with no one seeing the obvious? This man was a manipulative liar.

CHAPTER 14

Cornerstone—Vacationing in Hee Haw's Cornfield

Gloom, despair, and agony on me
Deep, dark depression, excessive misery
If it weren't for bad luck, I'd have no luck at all
Gloom, despair, and agony on me

Buck Owens and Roy Clark
From the TV show *Hee-Haw* (1969–1992)

God's plan is never clear-cut. I fear that most of us go through life trying to do what God wants, but never really knowing what God wants us to do. I think this is what causes most crises of faith. We think we are getting what God wants right, only to be met with the devastation of being on the wrong path. The question then becomes "How do you recover from questioning your faith?" You know God exists, so you are not in a crisis of faith situation just yet. However, you know if you do not find out what God's purpose is for you, a quick course correction on the path of life will not be all that is needed. You will have gone from questioning the meaning of your life to questioning the very existence of God at work in your life. These spiritual crises can freeze us in our state of mind. We become hopeless.

When going through my debilitating spiritual crisis, I found a dear friend who became a guide to keep my sanity. My friend said it may help my outlook if I immersed myself with positive reminders of God's presence. She said no matter where you go, or what you are doing, have some sort of reminder that God was right there beside you. She also said when she was going through rough spots, it helped her to overcome them by having a theme song. As she went through the day, she would hum the song in her head, imagining she was conquering the situation at hand. It could be any song that fit the situation. I could see her singing "Eye of the Tiger" from one of the *Rocky* movies as she dealt with her demons.

It was then that I found a few Christian rock stations on the car radio. It was just by chance. I did so much driving between all the school events, kids' activities, volunteer functions, therapy sessions, and the part-time sales job that it was a welcome relief. I found a daily theme song from this station.

Although the theme song approach did not take away my anger toward the situation, it did start an honest conversation with God. Between driving, singing, praying, and just being mad, I began to ask God and myself some very hard questions. The first was a series on *How am I supposed to survive with this man?* The questions ranged from *Was I just supposed to be a pushover and pray that we make it through to the other side?* to *How exactly am I supposed to leave him without a job, and why can't I find one?* Then came my favorites—the ones I feel like I will always ask myself. These were, *If I am supposed to be the arms and legs of the body of Christ, what is it that I am supposed to be doing?* and *Was God presenting me with tasks to do to elevate my situation and I just was missing them?*

My questions to God became more derogatory as my frustration grew. The dual therapies were becoming more convoluted as time went on. In addition, I started to have a feeling that my husband was just going through the motions at rehabilitation. My husband decided to plead not guilty for his public intoxication arrest because he was not given a breathalyzer. Out of anger I informed him that I would be present in court to make sure the court was aware that he had indeed been publicly drunk. The family therapist's stance on me going to the proceedings was "If you can't say anything nice, don't say anything at all." This perpetuated her do-nothing therapy.

I went to the public intoxication court proceedings because I was tired of being lied to. I also was at the financial point of going to the family priest for money to buy groceries and gas. Remember the one credit card that I used had been cut up? I still had no access to what used to be the joint checking account. I was totally dependent on my husband and the church for money to feed the kids as well as put gas in the car to get them to school. Every time I asked my husband for money, I was always given short of the amount I asked for, if any, and always in grocery certificates. We were living off the change from those grocery certificates.

When the court date came, I did not approach my husband in the courtroom; I just sat in the back. The lawyers made motions, and a large group of people were told to go to the clerk. My husband was in that group. I followed, not knowing if my husband would come back. I kept them in view so I would not lose them, but not close enough so I could hear. My husband went to several counters and finally ended up by the elevators with his lawyer. I again stayed close enough that I could see them, but not hear them. This upset the lawyer. He threw a tantrum, stating he would get the security office to have me thrown out of the public building. While the lawyer was stomping off, I said to my husband, "If you just tell me where and when you will meet me, I will go sit down." We agreed I would wait near the elevators. When he finally approached, I told him I needed money for food and gas, and he wrote a small check for one hundred dollars. We went our separate ways.

When this incident was brought up to the rehabilitation counselor, my husband said he was found not guilty and had to pay court costs. The counselor found this amusing and began to question him. He evaded the questions like "Do you know you were guilty?" and "What happens from there?" He literally looked at the floor and said, "I do not know" like a child. Finally, she turned to me and stated, "My understanding of these proceedings is, your husband had already served the maximum time in jail for the offense at the time of arrest. He needed to pay court costs, and possibly a fine, to complete the maximum sentence. After six months of being arrest free, he could expunge the arrest from his record." My husband did not know or just did not want to share this information.

As my husband's time at the rehabilitation treatment center began to wrap up, he and I had to attend a family therapy weekend at the center. This was required prior to my husband's release from outpatient rehabilitation. It was a three-day affair, 8:30 a.m. to 9:00 p.m. on Friday and Saturday and 9:00 a.m. to noon on Sunday. This weekend was supposed to allow us to bring our addict home into a loving positive environment because we are now battling a disease, not the person. The intent was to determine whether the patient had incorporated any of the therapy into their daily life, as well as to determine whether any of the wreckage from their home life had healed enough for them to return to a stable, loving environment. Throughout the weekend, the counselors supposedly watched interactions between family members to determine whether the patient was ready for release.

It was my understanding that it was also a time where I was supposed to use this time to get things off my chest, and I clarified this with rehabilitation therapist. We were supposed to let go of all the anger and accept the blanket apology from the addict for everything he or she had done wrong. I drove to the weekend events each day, so I used my friend's musical method to keep me going. I found singing a positive song in my head really helped.

There was a wide range of income levels represented as well as professions, but two main themes were common to all. Each addict openly admitted they stole, lied, and cheated for their addiction, and each family member just could not understand why they were not enough to satisfy the addict. There were approximately forty addicts, most with family members present. We were scheduled to meet in a large group as well as being broken up into groups that divided the addicts and nonaddicts.

There were many parents of alcoholics there. I openly commended this during our large group sessions on Friday and asked why parents could not come at other times, with alcoholism being so deep rooted. The rehabilitation center said they could, but it was up to the patient who they invited to come and when. When they asked a question about how I thought my husband's parents handled their son's condition, I said they just prayed but never got active. The center had many books on codependency; one that I read I felt offered instrumental advice on the subject. I recommended it to everyone during our large group time.

We covered a great deal of emotional ground in the small groups on Friday as well. The spouses at in our nonaddict group sessions said to me several times, "When you speak, he looks right through you. He looks at you but doesn't register a word." For instance, my husband did not consider him living out of the house as being "separated." The session ending with our group stating a blanket apology is not enough for our healing. One of the other wives said, "I want my husband to remember what he is apologizing for." Friday, although stressful, was an informative day. But unfortunately, the weekend was like being trapped in a bad country song.

As we moved through Saturday morning's large group session, I began feeling like I was in the middle of *Hee Haw*'s cornfield. *Hee Haw* was an old television show that was staged in a small town in the Deep South. The inhabitants usually ended up in a cornfield singing a song about how depressing their lives were. It occurred to me as I was listening to the addicts and their respective loved ones in this large group session that it was as if the miserable codependent family members had just realized there were other people just like them. The family members all had been lied to and taken advantage of. As a group they were all teary eyed and comparing notes. Consequently, all the lying addicts realized there was an equal number of miserable unlucky people lying to be happy. It sounded as if the addict crowd thought there were so many people in the same boat that it must be OK to do the lying in the first place. To me it sounded like these two groups sang in unison, "We are just the unluckiest, unloved people, and we are so glad that we found each other." In my head, I was beginning to see them all standing together holding hands and singing the *Hee Haw* cornfield theme song like "Kum Ba Yah."

My mind wandered off during this long Saturday session. I began to wonder if that *Hee Haw* song was what played in every addict's head as they went through their day tackling their issues.

During Saturday afternoon's large group session, there was a drawing exercise everyone was supposed to complete. On the front of the page, we were asked to color a tree and its roots. The tree itself was to portray what we showed to others as we lived our lives dealing with alcoholism. The roots part was to show what was actually occurring. On the back of that same page, we were supposed to draw a picture of what our future would be like after the family therapy weekend. Each addict and family member was supposed to complete this individually and present the picture to the large group.

I could not switch off the *Hee Haw* song that was playing in my head. It only played louder as I listened to the presentations. The addicts summarized their pictures about their lives, and each one just glossed over their details. They all could have just presented one picture. The front page for everyone was "I was bad, and I stole, but no one told me to stop, so I didn't. I lied, but no one cared, so I kept lying." On the back, most of the addicts had signs of fishing, and pretty fields of flowers symbolizing an "all healed, no-problem life." Not one person mentioned the work to get that problem-free life, though. The good life was just magically handed to them like a diploma at graduation as they were walking out of the treatment center.

Their family members' picture presentations also could have been one big collage. Each one said "We tried, but they would not listen to us. It was so awful having them around. There was nothing we could do." I kept waiting for something different to be said. As each new person spoke, the statements began to grate on my nerves; my frustration was at an all-time high. I found that I had waited until I was the last person to go.

When I spoke about my drawing, what people found was a very literal rendition of our home life. The tree itself was happy, good wife, good servant to the church. That is what people saw on the outside. However, the roots said that I was tired of being lied to, used for sex, verbally abused, made to beg for money, and I didn't want my kids to be driven around by a drunk. The back page of my drawing was also literal. I wanted functional family communication. If not, my husband would be out of the picture because the disease was killing him. I looked my husband straight in the eye and said, "If you are going to get sober, *now's the time!*"

I looked around the room at a bunch of wide-eyed people, codependent on each other.

I could not tell if they wanted me to shut up and sit down or continue with more earth-shattering information.

So I continued. "An addict's best friend for staying an addict is family members who don't let them feel the consequences from their behavior. The 'good lies' that you are telling to spare feelings were causing more harm than good."

Again, wide-eyed silence.

So I went on. I said, "It sounds like all of you are living in *Hee Haw*'s cornfield. You need to *move on.*"

Then people looked at me like they did not know what I was talking about.

Then I looked at some of the older generation and said, "You know, the theme song—it goes like this." And I sang:

> Gloom, despair, and agony on me
> Deep, dark depression, excessive misery
> If it weren't for bad luck, I'd have no luck at all
> Gloom, despair, and agony on me.

I was frustrated. I could not take any more drama. Right then and there I knew I wanted a divorce. I could not go through life in this particular cornfield!

My presentation closed the large group session. All of us family members were given a half-hour break out of the room. During the break, the restless addicts stayed in the room. My presentation started an addict revolt with my husband being the ringleader. He bonded with his peers by passing a petition, saying who wants to go to "my wife's treatment center?" Specialized counselors from the relapse recovery division were called in. Needless to say, addicts do not like being reminded of what they have done or what the future consequences would be. The Saturday session for the addicts turned into a chair-throwing brawl.

When relapse recovery division spoke to me to find out how long my husband had been drinking, they were in shock that he had not been caught before now. They said I had a right to be frustrated, but for my own personal safety I could not continue with the program that weekend. As I was leaving the center for the parking lot, I heard my husband say to a therapist, "I know my wife; she is angry, so she still cares. She would be indifferent if she did not care." The therapist stated, "She is downright mad, and I can tell this is your last chance." My husband said he was through with drinking. But remember, these were the people who decided whether my husband was ready to leave the program.

As I drove to pick up the kids, I did not know whether to feel vindicated or believing I had caused my husband's drinking problems. I just knew I was done caring. Let's face it, life is work; there is no escaping it. Each day people without addictions have work to do and choices to make. Sometimes, life is not all about having fun or lying about having fun, so you don't end up with the consequences later on. Regardless of what the people during that weekend thought of me, I knew you just could not play a bad country song backward and have all the repercussions from an addict's life resolved. The addicts needed to go back down the rabbit hole that they were in, retracing their steps and picking up the pieces of their lost souls along the way. There is no skip-ahead card like in UNO, or magic slide like in Candy Land that allows people to skate around life lessons.

The next weekend my husband had a visitation day on Saturday when he could come to the house. Nothing was mentioned about the previous weekend. It was a low-key visit from what I remember. It was like the man I had married was back. My husband hung around as long as he could. When it was my husband's time to leave, the kids and I were being goofy during a TV show they like to watch. There was a look about my husband when he left. The same look I had learned about the weekend before at the therapy weekend. It was the look when he is struggling with his addiction; it was written all over his face. Before he left, I casually told him I could see "that look," which was supposed to be a high sign to him that he needed a stronger focus on sobriety. However, my husband drank while he drove to the halfway house. His housemates caught him, and he was admitted into the inpatient program pending insurance approval.

I just could not believe that after that whole *Hee Haw* weekend experience he learned nothing. Don't you have to use the tools that God places before you? Wasn't this the part of the path where my husband had to retrace his steps to regain his soul? Don't you have to want to change and not lose what you have? Shouldn't you have to love your family more than you love alcohol and lying? Apparently, my husband did not think so; he thought he was above all of that.

He was scheduled to stay at the rehab inpatient facility while we waited for the insurance to be approved. I was given the tasks of finding his car, giving him his belongings, and finding the bills at his work. My husband gave me a check for $2,500 and told me to "pay as many of the bills as you can." I informed him that this probably would not cover all of them, but that I could put groceries and gas on a credit card that I had opened for emergencies until we got it figured out. He agreed, I thought, and I went on my way feeling like we were a team. He seemed lucid and ready to change. When the insurance company denied my husband's claim, my husband called for me to come pick him up on Monday at 10:00 p.m. I felt upset at him, but we had just had a great weekend day with the kids. He was like the man I loved. I did not hesitate in going to pick him up. I had no choice but to take the kids with me when I went to pick him up. There was no one around to keep them.

Getting inpatient rehabilitation covered was a battle in paperwork. My husband tried to get help from our primary care doctor with the insurance. Going through the infertility process, I knew the insurance appeal steps well. It is just a part of the insurance process. I asked if he wanted me to help, and he said yes.

Later that day, when he returned from his appointment with the family counselor, my husband had changed his mind. He said the family counselor wanted him to be responsible for his own recovery. I called the rehabilitation center and discussed the hands-off approach to getting someone into inpatient treatment. They thought my husband just needed to appeal the process with clear information, and he would be admitted. They stated that I should give as much assistance as I could. However, with my husband being back to his violent, manipulative self, I had no choice but to honor his request and do nothing. In the end, my husband had decided to complete the twelve-step process with his sponsor and go to AA every night. His rationale was that is what he would be doing when he left the rehabilitation center anyway. Then my husband began to deny that he told me to pay as many of the bills as I could with the money. He said I should have saved money for food and gas and that I was irresponsible.

Shortly after my husband was kicked out of rehabilitation, I left the family counseling therapy, taking the kids out as well. The family counselor had convinced my husband that I was to blame for all his drinking, the kids' stress, and all the problems in the marriage. My husband had manipulated the system to control perception of the truth, finances, and the kids' love. Nothing had changed. It had just gotten increasingly covert.

CHAPTER 15

For God Is Not a God of Confusion but of Peace

(1 Cor 14:33)[26]

If the unbelieving spouse walks out, you've got to let him or her go. You don't have to hold on desperately. God has called us to make the best of it, as peacefully as we can. (1 Cor 7:15)[27]

God never provides an easy, clear-cut solution to a problem. I thought the rehabilitation center was the answer to my prayers; however, our home life continued to spiral downward. I had to find a way of divorcing this man for safety's sake. He did not want to change, and unfortunately, he was such a slick liar that he had manipulated everyone's perception of the situation. He had only one repercussion from his public intoxication charge and that was losing his government clearance to work on the secure Department of Energy property. I felt this would serve as a big wake-up call to him, but he and his lawyer had plans to regain his clearance. So, there I sat, with no job, a husband who drank profusely, and fear keeping me feeling frozen and powerless in this situation.

I thought my experience was beyond my control. But in reality, I was avoiding taking responsibility for making decisions and solving problems. I wanted God to just take care of it. I wanted to pray it away. What I did not realize at that moment was that God was waiting for me to wake up and move on.

While I didn't know what to do, I refused to believe God wanted me to stay with this man. I knew enough scripture to find this verse and recite it over and over.

> Don't become partners with those who reject God. How can you make a partnership out of right and wrong? That's not a partnership; that's war. Are light and dark best friends? Does Christ go strolling with the Devil? Do trust and mistrust hold hands? Who would think of setting up pagan idols in God's holy Temple? But that is exactly what we are, each of us a temple in whom God lives. God himself put it this way: "I'll live in them, move into them; I'll be their God and they'll be my people. So leave the corruption and compromise; leave it for good," says God. "Don't link up with those who will pollute you. I want you all to myself. I'll be a Father to you; you'll be sons and daughters to me." The Word of the Master, God. (2 Cor 6:14)[28]

While I recited, I begged God to do something. I knew I did not have to stay married to the man my husband had become. But I clung to the thought that the way I handled this situation might bring my husband not only back to us but to God. In my heart of hearts, I still wanted God to heal my family. I wanted my kids to have their sober father back. I wanted to see the man I married again. And I knew that God had the power to use any situation for good.

God's answer came approximately three weeks after my husband was removed from the rehabilitation center.

When his father called at 12:30 a.m. on a Monday night, I asked if there was an emergency. When he said no, I told him it was too late to be calling and hung up on him.

This is when I found my husband in bed with me.

We agreed that he was sleeping on the couch until he found another halfway house. When I tried to confront my husband, he ignored me. I decided to hold my ground and insisted he honor that agreement. This is when my husband proceeded to choke me and beat me. After an array of physical and verbal abuse, my husband left the room. I locked the door, holding the lock and the doorknob so he could not pick the lock as usual. I stood at the door like this for two hours. When he tried to reenter the bedroom, I put my full weight against the door, holding tightly to the door handle.

When he was unsuccessful after several tries, he left to call his father in Kentucky. I could hear my husband say, "Everything is fine." This statement made my blood boil. Things were far from fine, and I was tired of my husband lying to his parents. I picked up the bedroom extension telling his father what had occurred and apologized for hanging up on him earlier in the evening. I said my husband obviously needed to talk to him about something. I proceeded to say that I had enough marks on me to prove physical abuse. I hung up the extension, going back to hold the door and waited for the house to be quiet. I heard my husband say, "Don't worry, Dad; I didn't hurt her that bad."

When the conversation with his dad ended, he went downstairs to sleep on the couch. It was then that I called a friend down the street to take pictures of the marks. She took pictures, and we found my husband passed out on the couch downstairs. The kids slept, I think, through the whole process. This one documentable incident set my release from this man in motion.

The next day, I called the family priest, who instructed me to file for an order of protection. I called around for lawyers. I also proceeded to make plans with my friend to be safe. Since the four of us were friends, I asked this couple to facilitate a discussion on boundaries, thinking maybe a different voice would get my husband to understand what he was doing. She and her husband came down that evening when my husband returned from work. Our goal was to come up with some sort of living arrangement he would agree to that others would witness. Something where there was some sort of accountability.

We talked about a deadbolt lock on the bedroom door. My husband refused to allow my friend's husband to put it on. I was back to being the patient warrior, hoping we could use God's prescribed plan of communication for resolving the conflict. Our friends came up with an idea. Both my husband and I should come up with a list of boundaries for the other to adhere to. We agreed. Each of us was to present our lists to the wife, then we would proceed as a group to discuss each other's list and work on a common boundary game plan. My husband had four "complaints" and my list was more operational. Although my husband agreed that my items were technically boundaries, he said he was not agreeing to honor any of them.

Stonewalling was his game from then on.

When I found a lawyer from our church on Wednesday, he stated that I needed someone in the medical field to document the bruising. On the Thursday of that week, I met with my gynecologist. He documented the bruising scheduling me for an emergency mammogram to determine how deep the damage went. In addition, he scheduled me for a hysterectomy. With the potential to be without insurance, I begged my gynecologist to schedule the hysterectomy surgery as soon as possible. By chance, there was an opening for the next week.

When I informed the lawyer of the hysterectomy, he stated that I needed to be free of painkillers before I could go to court for an order of protection. That meant that I had to keep the plan for the court order a secret, living under the same roof as my husband. However, God provided a solution to this problem as best as he could.

On Friday, the next day, my husband's parents were coming to town to spend some time with their grandkids. They had rented a hotel room where there was a pool so everyone could swim. Like most times when his father called or came for a visit, my husband went slightly off the deep end. The evening started fine as we were getting ready for their arrival. I was cleaning and cooking, and my husband was in and out running errands. The night took a turn for the worse when the verbal abuse started to run rampant. I would not let my husband harass me. I would turn my back and do something else while he was yelling at me. He was intimidating, barring me from leaving the bedroom. He pulled the phone out of the wall in one of his tirades. Then he stated he was going to take our son for baseball sign-ups, and he would not bring our son home. His plan was to just leave a seven-year-old at the sign-up facility. Remembering indifference is the worst you can do to an abusive person, I said goodbye. And I prayed for a safe return.

When the two returned home, our son and I started to clean his guinea pig cage. My husband started his tirade again. This time when met with indifference and I said, "You're crossing a boundary" repeatedly, my husband went to slap me. He stopped short of my face and said, "See, I know when to stop." He proceeded to call 911. He told the dispatcher that I wanted to talk to them. All of this was in front of our son.

When my husband handed me the phone, I told the person that I had not asked him to call. I continued to say that my husband was an alcoholic, and he was confrontational but had not hit me yet that night. Currently, he was just verbally abusive and that I knew there was nothing they could do. My husband told me to give him the phone. He told them not to worry; he was leaving and going to his brother's in town, giving them the number where he could be reached. He hung up and left.

About five minutes later, he returned more agitated than before. As the verbal abuse continued, I realized there was no point in waiting. I called 911 to have him removed. When the police arrived, one of the officers was one who had arrested my husband on for public intoxication, the charge that woke him up and put him in rehabilitation. He and his partner sorted out our stories and proceeded to tell my husband he was either going to jail or staying with relatives. That was the last night he spent in the house. My husband tried calling the hotel where his parents were staying, but they had not checked in yet.

We found my husband's parents visiting with their other son in town. The police talked to my husband's dad, stating my husband needed to be removed from the premises. He was not being allowed to drive himself because the officer smelled alcohol.

When my father-in-law arrived Friday night, I asked him if he wanted to see the pictures from Monday. I wanted him to have a clear, unbiased picture of what had transpired. He said yes, asking if he could keep one to show my husband's mom. I agreed because I know they have a hard time trying to figure out the truth from 300 miles away. I also told my father-in-law that his son alluded that I did not want my children to see them over the weekend. I wanted to make it clear that the kids wanted to swim with them, and I was in no way planning to change that regardless of the circumstances. I further clarified that it was me who did not want to see them. I continued with the kids' and my morning plans so we could work out pickup arrangements. My husband left with his dad after trying to give the police and me a signed statement saying he had not been drinking that evening. The following day he told me his two mistakes were drinking liquor in the backseat of his car and calling 911.

I spoke to my mother-in-law on Saturday. I told her that although I realized that they did not know what to do, some of their behavior was enabling the drinking to continue. Comments on the telephone like "You don't sound drunk" and "You don't look like you have been drinking" only continued the charade of normalcy. I told them I was seeing an Al-Anon group that I chose specifically to understand them, the parents of grown alcoholics. I ended with that it would be wise if they went to Al-Anon so they could figure out how to talk to their son and not perpetuate the "everything is fine" game. I told her that every time they came to town, my husband's stress level was out of control. I also told her that although this situation made me angry, it probably hurt her probably more than me because she was his mother. She said, "There are some things I still don't believe."

I continued with the surgery the following week as a "no information patient." That is a patient who has no information in the front desk computer, so if people call about them, no information can be given out. A dear friend dropped me off at the hospital on the way to work, returning for me on a lunch break the next day. During my downtime, the children stayed with the neighbors, and lovely people brought me food. After the painkillers were no longer needed, but before I could drive, my children came home, and people carted them to and from school as well as brought food and did laundry. Through the whole ordeal, my neighbor provided midnight walks for my dog. More people continued my volunteer functions, the children's liturgy ministry at my parish, sewing costumes for the school's grandparents day musical, and delivering Girl Scout cookies. Most people helping had no idea of my true circumstances.

During this time, my husband found a halfway house with an outpatient program. He also convinced the people at this halfway house, as well as at work, that I needed him to take care of the family while I was recuperating from my hysterectomy. He had a doctor at a health clinic sign paperwork so that he could have family leave. I suppose these actions looked good to people looking at our situation from the outside. They provided a great backdrop for getting his clearance back. But everyone knows that character means doing what's right when nobody's looking.

On my first full day home, my husband was in and out of the house. He stood at the end of the bed on different occasions and yelled at me. I did nothing, mostly pretended to be asleep. The neighbor keeping the kids stated he was in and out of her house as well. He did not knock when he entered that house, he just walked right in the front door until she started locking it. While he was there, he shouted at the kids a lot. She told him that he is no longer welcome in her home and not to come by to see the kids at all. He would not be let in.

During the weeks in between my surgery and my follow-up appointment, I tried to stay very quiet. People still brought food in knowing that I could not drive. On Fridays, my husband would come and eat everything that was in the refrigerator that people had left for the kids and me. His arrogance filled the house. It was Lent before I was finally able to drive. My husband used this to reduce the amount of food allowance again, saying that he did not need to pay for meals on Fridays; the church served a Lenten dinner.

Two weeks before Easter, my husband had his scheduled time with the family counselor he was still seeing. After that meeting, around two o'clock, my husband showed up at the house. The kids and I were trying to build a guinea pig cage outside. He sat in a lawn chair and criticized us, and he yelled at the children to "finish with your mother; she is obviously more important than me." Our son started to act out and spray weed killer on the lawn. In addition, he turned on the sprinkler and began to run through it, something I had told him not to do several times that day already. My husband responded by saying, "Your mother is just trying to control you like everything else."

At this point, I stated that I had an hour of errands to run. My husband said he had to leave in forty-five minutes. I said I would be back in forty-five minutes, but when I returned, he stayed for additional thirty minutes. During this time, our son was watching TV and our daughter was sitting on his lap outside. My husband was trying to get her to speak about school events. I finally said we needed to leave for the Lenten dinner. I was thankful that the next day I had an appointment to visit my gynecologist. I was cleared for everything but heavy lifting. I filed for an order of protection through the family crisis unit with my attorney. God had provided a way out of this marriage. I knew that God did not want me to stay with this man. There was nothing God could do to bend his free will. He wanted to drink more than he wanted anything else. I was physically and mentally ready for battle, or so I thought.

When my husband was served with the order of protection a few days later, he came into the house and yelled at me for two hours. Since the order was not formalized by a judge, it was just applied for, my husband did not have to honor the agreement yet. I had no recourse but to listen to his rant while I tried not to make the situation worse. I tried to explain to him that he never hears the words that I say. I said, "I am indifferent to your disease, I want to be alone. It is time for you to leave; I can no longer take this physically or emotionally. I do not want to see you or hear from you." I said I did not know if it was because he did not have sisters, a good role model for husbands, or what the problem was, but he just could not communicate with the female gender. I wanted to be left alone so I could heal. Nothing sank in. I began to have pain in my chest and told him, "I have to lie down now—leave." When I picked the kids up from school on that same day, I talked with the principal of the school, apologizing for our stress and reminding her that until the court proceedings, we had no parenting plan in place. Each of us had our own right to do whatever we wanted, and I would try not to get the school in the middle. I assured her that my husband, on his good days, would also do the same because it was the disease, not the person, that causes problems.

The timing of the order of protection was difficult for two reasons. first, it was six weeks after the attack. However, both the crisis unit and my lawyer stated this was not an issue; it could easily be explained by my need for the hysterectomy. The second reason was it was my son's first Communion. With an order of protection, my husband could not come to dinner with us after the events at the church. I felt bad for my son because his special day was compromised. For his sister's first Communion two years prior, we threw a party with our friends and family in attendance. Now, all those friends were no longer a part of our lives; they had been worn out by the alcoholic tirades. At my son's special day, the only people in attendance were my parents, who came from Michigan. Although the choice I made diminished my son's event, I knew had I not stood up for myself, the beatings would increase. During my parent's stay, my husband left several phone messages, including one that said, "I will fight you; I will give no money. I thought we had an agreement that I would stay away from you. What you have done prohibits me from seeing the kids." I found each statement interesting because the order of protection was very clearly written and provided for time with the kids.

CHAPTER 16

Detach with Love

I am speaking the truth in Christ—I am not lying;
my conscience bears me witness in the Holy Spirit.
(Rom 9:1 ESV)[29]

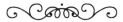

My lawyer felt it was imperative that we allow the kids to have time with their father; he said it would look poorly on me in court if I denied his parental rights. I agreed to supervised exchange with our friends who had tried to help with the boundary discussions until we could get supervised visitation though the court. My husband took the kids to Easter service and was going to make any other Easter plans that he could. Knowing my husband had nowhere to take the kids and that I didn't want them to be in the car with him, I suggested they have Easter at the house. My husband took the kids to 10 a.m. mass at the parish where we were members and returned home for an Easter dinner of pizza. I went to Easter mass at the parish where my kids went to school. It was a difficult mass to sit through, as I wondered if my children were safe from drunk driving. To keep my mind occupied, I began to people watch in church.

It was during my people watching that I witnessed the kind of relationship that I wanted to have. I saw a husband giving communion to his wife, and the look in their eyes was beautiful. I asked God why I couldn't have that type of relationship. It's all that I had ever wanted. I asked myself, *Did God present me with one before I met my spouse, and I just did not take the opportunity?* Was it possible that God could heal my husband of alcoholism and we could still have the type of relationship where you are a team? After all, isn't that God's plan for a marriage, where each person helps the other become the best inside and out? Where you stand up for each other, not letting an outside influence harm either person? Was that God's plan for us, and was God using the order of protection as a wake-up call to my husband?

I sat there and watched this loving couple, longing to be loved like that. What I did not realize was that this type of thinking was the stumbling block that was not allowing me to move forward. I had an unrealistic view of what God was trying to do with my marriage. God could not provide me a way out of the abuse and a perfect marriage at the same time. I was reading a book about the hidden abuse that indicated this Cinderella view of marriages was a leading cause of domestic violence in my family's income bracket.[30] I often wonder if I had read the book earlier if I would have made the same mistakes.

When I returned home at the designated exchange time of 5:00 p.m., my husband was not ready. He said he was using a clock that was an hour behind. He put on a big show for everyone with tearful goodbyes. When I asked the kids what they did during their time with their dad, they said they chose one board game each to play with him (a total of two hours), then he watched TV while the kids played in their rooms for the remainder of the time.

My husband requested, through our friends, that he take the kids to 10:00 a.m. mass and out to lunch the following Sunday. I reminded him that I would be leading children's liturgy at that time and did not want him at mass. It is what I do for the church; it is my ministry. The program is stressful enough without having to coordinate handoffs or making sure we didn't run into each other. I said he could go to one of the other masses and have the kids however it worked out, but for the next two Sundays, and starting again in fall, 10:00 a.m. masses were off-limits. I was told by our friends to have the kids in the narthex at

11:00 a.m. and that was that. I had no information on when they were coming home or how.

At 11:00 a.m., I sent the kids from the parish hall where I was leading the children's liturgy mass to the narthex. Seven minutes later, while dealing with parents in the parish hall, I saw my husband standing on the sidewalk to the church just staring at me with his hands on his hips, no children in sight. He stood there for about five minutes while I talked with families. He spoke to no one; he just stood there watching me with his hand on his hips. When a friend walked by me, I told her to tell my husband that the kids were inside of the church. She said, "He knows; I saw them getting doughnuts together after mass." I asked, "Where are they now?" She said she did not know.

Later that afternoon, our friends who were supervising the exchanges of the kids called, saying I needed to come down the street to pick them up. When I arrived, I was informed that the same arrangement for next week would be occurring, but at 10:00 a.m. mass instead of the 11:15 a.m. one. My husband was going to 10:00 a.m. mass, taking the kids to lunch, and he wasn't sure about the drop-off. I reiterated my problem with that mass—that I am everywhere. I was told that the information would be passed along. This signaled the times to come. My husband made the rules with no regard to the order of protection boundaries. No one could enforce what was on paper or what was agreed to verbally.

Our court date to formalize the order of protection arrived. The night prior to court I had a short dream that my lawyer was holding me on his lap like a child. I was very small, my head down on his shoulder, sitting almost lifeless. When I woke up in a cold sweat, I realized that my lawyer held a great deal of power over my life and the lives of my children. I was at the mercy of his skill and intellect.

Before I filed into the courthouse with my lawyer, I read a page from the Al-Anon handbook. It had become my custom to read the book prior to any dealings with my husband, so I took Al-Anon book everywhere, reading it before leaving the car. In bold letters the page said DETACH. This should have been a signal that anything that was about to happen was not personal, but part of God's plan. Little did I know that my husband had spent the time he should have been playing with the kids searching for dirt against me on the computer. The only items that even existed were the letters to the family priest on my computer, which he printed off. I often wonder if the family therapist put him up to it.

When his lawyer presented these letters to my lawyer, the battle quickly changed. My lawyer was upset, telling me, "Look what you have done to me; if you go into court, you will lose your children." I thought, *What I had done to him? How about what my husband had done to me?* My lawyer went on to say that his grandfather was an alcoholic, and he wasn't that bad to be around. In my state of mind, it seemed to me that my lawyer was trying to make it appear that I was making a bigger deal of my husband's drinking than I needed to. He said I needed to distance myself from the church, stop writing everything down, and to make sure I was not a controlling person. He said he wanted me in a therapist's office, and he wanted to choose the therapist. He wanted psychological evaluations, and he wanted to choose the evaluator. I felt genuinely guilty for not giving the letters to him. I felt confused at how my husband could be so cruel. I told my lawyer to call the priest and ask for his help. Flatly refusing, he said, "Priests do not need to be bothered with situations like this."

As the proceedings ensued, I ended up with the injunction that the kids had to see the family therapist even though I had pulled them out because of the therapist's abusive techniques. In addition, I received an injunction that would not allow me to speak to priests, because in my husband's view, I was painting him in a bad light. But let's not stop there—my husband was also seeking full custody and stated that I owed him alimony from my share of the marital estate. His reasoning was that I was mentally unstable based on the letters he had pulled off the computer, and the kids were in jeopardy. My lawyer set up a psychological evaluator for my husband and me, stating he was the best in town. Somehow this was now a battle for my sanity, not a clear and simple divorce. I continued to ask myself, *How can my husband be so good at manipulating his version of the truth? How can he get away without having consequences? Why doesn't God give him any consequences?*

My lawyer pursued the order of protection issues. He floundered with what to do with my husband's choice of keeping the kids with the family counselor and did not do anything to keep the other side from stonewalling on whatever they wanted. My lawyer was difficult to get ahold of and even worse with getting anything accomplished or even communicating his plan. I was frustrated at feeling like I had to keep up the documentation mode. I had to think of outcomes to the legal game and present them to him. I just could not understand what I was paying for.

Looking back at this time I could see how in God's mysterious way he was trying to show me who my husband really was. Although I had lived honestly, I had lived my life with blinders on. I truly believed that God could cure anything; however, in my husband's case, he did not want to be cured. No consequences or counseling would make him want to stop drinking because he did not believe he had a problem. God wanted me to move on with my life without him because I deserved something better. I read somewhere that we all must be the betrayed and the betrayer at some point. We need to be both for perspective; we must feel each side before the soul can move on. Any soul that gets stuck will repeat the same behavior.

In thinking of this statement, I had certainly been betrayed, but I wondered when I had been the betrayer. Nothing I had ever done equaled this treatment. One thing was for sure. I was no longer a trusting soul. I determined that I no longer wanted just an order of protection from this man; I wanted a divorce. Even if he stopped drinking, I knew I could never trust him again. I had learned the truth. I returned to searching books for a way to cope with my situation.

I wanted to be always surrounded by truth. I did not want to hear hopeful supposing's from well-wishers. I did not want people to freeze up when I came around, not knowing if they should tell me they saw my husband out drinking.

Sarah Erstwhile

It was such a sad time for me. Now I had to gather witnesses for my defense, which meant trying to teach my friends and parish members that the truth is something that is solid and unshakeable. You cannot be embarrassed by telling the truth. Unfortunately, my husband's mean spirit attacking the truth made people not want to get involved. Despite my efforts, I could not get people to understand that when something important is going on, silence is a lie (A. M. Rosenthal).[31] People began to steer clear of our family situation. My friends' ignorance about the importance speaking up may have derailed a speedy divorce, but in the end, the truth was always on my side.

CHAPTER 17

Faith Is the Opposite of Doubt

Anyone who meets a testing challenge head-on and manages to stick it out is mighty fortunate. For such persons loyally in love with God, the reward is life and more life. Don't let anyone under pressure to give in to evil say, "God is trying to trip me up." God is impervious to evil and puts evil in no one's way. The temptation to give in to evil comes from us and only us. We have no one to blame but the leering, seducing flare-up of our own lust. Lust gets pregnant, and has a baby: sin! Sin grows up to adulthood and becomes a real killer. (Jas 1:12–15)[32]

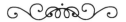

The major reason the divorce was not over sooner was the fact I had written letters to my priest about my feelings toward God's presence. My husband pulled them off the computer and gave them to his lawyer, and the battle started. I became angry at God; it was not me who wanted to write everything down, but it was what I was asked to do. Because of this, my lawyer thought I was a ridiculous woman.

During the years leading up to the divorce, one positive thing did happen. I became closer to God. Of course, he did not give me what I wanted, but I at least felt closer to some sort of guidance and protection, however convoluted it may be. Each night I would pray, "I just want to get back home to you. I don't want to be lost anymore; just find me wherever I am. Please just find me, God."

When I finally got a new, secure job, I called my lawyer and plainly stated that his comments about his alcoholic grandfather seemed to me like he was trying to influence my decisions. I went on to say that I did not want to hear about the grandfather anymore. A day later I received a letter stating he no longer wanted to be my lawyer. I remember when I received the letter firing me from being his client. The letter stated that I had lost faith in him, and he in me. I opened it in the early morning at my new job.

What a blow. Say what is on your mind and get kicked to the curb. This left me with no lawyer and a husband who felt he could do anything he wanted. I had a new job, one I knew nothing about, and I had to go hunt down a lawyer so I could not lose my kids.

My goal was to learn from my past. Maybe I failed to do everything required to make the lawyer's job easy. I know God has a plan for everyone, and not everyone is meant to finish what they start. Each of us has better strengths. Maybe my last lawyer's only function was getting the process started and keeping me from looking like the peculiar church lady. Maybe the whole process was to take what I learned and to make a good choice in lawyers the second time around.

I remember the hunt for a new lawyer. It was devastatingly brutal. I had to find a new lawyer fast before my husband and his lawyer found out. I called a friend that was a divorce attorney; her firm had no room for me. She gave me a list of names, and I went from there. Out of six, only one answered the phone and made an appointment. I juggled all of this while training for a new job. A job I had sought for three years.

When I got to my appointment, I told her who my husband's attorney was; she stated the case would be too time-consuming for her. It was then that I found out my husband found his lawyer in AA My husband was his only client at the time. This lawyer was not even a divorce lawyer, but he sure knew how to make trouble.

She was kind enough to give me six more names. I went back to work and called the names the next morning. By some miracle, the first lawyer I called answered the phone and made an appointment for the next week. I called the other five to set up more appointments and no one answered.

I cashed the only retirement account I had, and with $12,000, I was ready for the next week's meeting. All of this sounds minor. However, I was doing all of this while driving the kids to and from a school that was in a different town, dealing with their emotions about the divorce and the psychologist, cooking, cleaning, doing laundry, going to and from after-school events, and training for a job that I truly knew nothing about. Plus, I could not leave work until 5:45 p.m., and the kids needed to be picked up twenty minutes away. How I managed was by the grace of God.

I scheduled the lawyer appointment at 8:00 a.m., enough time to get the kids to school at 7:15 a.m. and drive thirty miles in the opposite direction to the meeting. I remember getting out of the car praying that this one would understand me and protect me. He was professional and organized. I gave him everything, including my letters to the priest. I prayed before I went in and prayed as I was going to work thirty minutes later. I made it to work on time at 9:00 a.m. for more training.

This is when I realized that it is important for everyone to have someone they trust to bounce ideas off. It is equally important for everyone to trust their own judgment. I wish growing up I had someone who I could bounce stuff off to develop better judgment. I lived secluded; I didn't learn how people could be when they did not think of others first. I think that is where most of us get into trouble—we just haven't learned how to deal with another person's manipulative thinking. Without this expertise, we end up embroiled in years of heartache learning how to handle adults playing childish games.

That is where lawyers come in. Lawyers become the sticks and stones used in adult fighting. You cannot survive an alcoholic husband acting like an angst-ridden teenager without a good lawyer. Lawyers know all the rules and how to document the fight properly. They know when to speak and what will give the other side a chance to mess up. I feel sorry that my first lawyer wasn't up to the challenge of handling all the antics and stonewalling. Looking back, he enabled my husband. He let my husband think everything was OK; he did not get dinged for noncompliance. Maybe that was his plan—to lull him into thinking everything was fine. However, it did not teach my husband boundaries; it merely gave away ground. Much of this ground my second lawyer had to combat.

My first lawyer left me feeling that we were not doing everything we could to properly document the lies swirling around the divorce. My second lawyer was all about the documentation. He reaffirmed my belief that we are doing all that we can. My second lawyer had the playbook; he was honest with me and fair. He took the time to explain what I didn't understand. He was the big brother I always wanted, even if he wasn't my close friend. I felt if we failed, I knew it would not be on us but the system. It would be God's plan, not our mistake. My only complaint was that the process is so expensive and unpredictable.

I begged God to let this one protect me and my children. I thanked God that the opposing side never found out I was without a lawyer for three weeks. Through the course of the divorce, not once did my new lawyer ever answer the phone again. Regardless of the number of times I called, or the time the calls were placed, I always reached the receptionist. The timing of the first call was just one of those moments where God made things happen.

CHAPTER 18

There Are Two Things That Kill the Soul: Despair and False Hope[33]

—Saint Augustine

Despair is not just an emotion, in a deeper sense it is the loss of self.[34]
—Anti-Climacus, from *The Sickness unto Death*

Hope is the belief in a positive outcome related to events and circumstances in one's life. Hope is different from positive thinking, which refers to a systematic process used for reversing pessimism. The term false hope refers to a hope based entirely around a fantasy or an extremely unlikely outcome.[35]
—*The American Heritage Dictionary of the English Language*, 4th ed.

It takes a great deal of pain to kill a truly religious soul. Although I had been through a great deal of pain, I still hoped God would prevail. I knew he would provide me with a custody arrangement that would protect my children, as well as a divorce agreement that would not leave me destitute. There was much to be done. First and foremost was to get the kids away from the abusive family therapist. Next were the psychological evaluations to determine who was the most mentally sound parent. Afterward, there needed to be four mediation sessions where both sides would try to hammer out an agreement prior to the court date. If the parents could not come to a deal, a trial would take place. I was hopeful that regardless of how I was now viewed as a controlling church lady, I would be viewed as the better parent. After all what is worse—too much church or too much alcohol?

I gave all the documents to my new lawyer. We had already been over the high points of the case; I did not give him much verbal input so as not to color his view of what needed to be done with the divorce proceedings. He was genuinely shocked when he found that I had an injunction against me prohibiting me to talk to priests. He stated it was an illegal injunction. However, there was a positive to the injunction; no one could accuse me of manipulating the priests' view of my husband.

My lawyer also could not believe the amount of money that had already been spent with and how little was accomplished. We later discovered the problem. My husband's lawyer would call or show up at the previous lawyer's office intoxicated with no apparent goal for the call or visit. The same behavior began again with the new lawyer.

Regardless, the two lawyers hammered away at each other. Eventually, through meetings in the judge's chambers, the two lawyers resolved the injunction as well as who would be the kids' therapist. Unfortunately, the new therapist had her work cut out for her; neither child would talk to her, especially my daughter. Her taste for therapy was soured given the treatment from the last therapist.

When it came to the psychological evaluations, things were a bit more challenging. We each had to take a battery of tests and there were interviews with the school and friends. Then there were home visits to my home and to his apartment, both scheduled while the kids were there. One would think that this could be accomplished in a month or so. But a quick resolution was not to be. The evaluator's family became ill, not once but twice. In addition, my husband found a girlfriend in AA. This girlfriend had two high-school-aged daughters whom my children were in awe of. There seemed to be no boundaries when it came to my parenting time. The girls called my home late at night. Little did I know that my soon-to-be ex-husband was telling the girls to call and check on the children. Then the girlfriend started visiting the school. She showed up unannounced during my parenting time without their father. If there was a special event in the classroom, she was there, not him.

Next were the camping trips with their alcohol and drug treatment group. When I brought this to the attention of the children's new therapist, I learned something disturbing. This new girlfriend had lost custody of her girls and she only had them on the weekends that my husband had ours. My children's therapist had testified in court as the evaluator who recommended her children be taken away. As I inquired more about this girlfriend through many sources, I found she was best friends with my husband's lawyer from AA; she slipped into my husband's life right when we were examining the financial standing of our divorce case.

When I discussed this with the kids' therapist, I received a warning that this lady had no boundaries or fear. I mentioned this to the psychological evaluator when it was time for one of our meetings. I wanted it recorded for the court that she was now in my kids' life, having already lost the custody of her children. If she was going to be a part of my kids' life, I wanted her sanity evaluated.

He questioned her, and then there we sat, waiting for the evaluator to write the report. For eight months we waited. During those eight months, a great deal happened. My husband and his new girlfriend decided she needed to become Catholic through the parish where I led the children's liturgy program. Even though she had been married twice before and was sleeping with a married man, they began the process. This led to her showing up at my children's liturgy program on occasion to see my children. She told me since we were going to be parish members together, I should just get used to it.

When I brought this to the attention of the therapist, she stated that I should screen my daughter's email. I obtained the passwords and sure enough, my daughter had started to receive emails concerning me from this woman. It was a barrage of communication degrading my parenting style. Her opinion was that kids should be allowed to do what they wanted without hassling from their parents. When my daughter told her father that she gave the password to me, he set up a different account for her. The situation came to a head when I stopped off at the parish to drop off posters for an upcoming program one day. I had the kids with me, even though it was a school day. Both kids had head colds, and we were coming back from the pediatrician's office. Since it was on our way home, we stopped into the parish. When we walked into the narthex to tape up the posters, who should follow in after us but the girlfriend. She was full of questions about the kids being out of school. I remained composed, knowing any type of communication would be manipulated. I felt like I was being stalked.

I made an appointment to discuss this with the priest. When I spoke to him, however, it was his opinion that it would be best if I found another parish. His reasoning was that my spiritual well-being was in danger, and that they needed this parish more than I did. I was quite shocked. Here I had served this parish for more than ten years in a very visible ministry role. I was even writing portions of the liturgy program when the wording was not written for preschoolers to understand. Through the years I had been loyal, diligently making sure each child understood the value of being a Christian. I left the meeting feeling discarded. Once my shock disappeared, I thought long and hard about the motivation behind my husband and his new girlfriend wanting to be at the parish that I put so much time in. It was more for appearance's sake than spirituality. They wanted to report to the evaluator that I had left the church, and that I could not get along with them. I decided to stay with the parish and in charge of the children's liturgy program until the psychological evaluations were through and the custody agreement had been determined.

For several months I carried on a children's liturgy program for seventy-five families without guidance from the priest. To make matters worse, I had no spiritual guidance as to how to deal with my divorce.

CHAPTER 19

The Injustices of Life

I also noticed that under the sun there is evil in the courtroom. Yes, even the courts of law are corrupt! I said to myself, "In due season God will judge everyone, both good and bad, for all their deeds. (Eccl 7:16–17)[36]

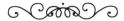

While we were waiting for the evaluator to write his report, my lawyer and I began to sift through the financial documents. When I went in for our scheduled appointment, I figured it would be a short conversation. But it was then that I found out the vile ways of my husband.

My lawyer drew columns on the white board in his conference room, one with my name on it and one with my husband's name. His first listed the obvious assets—the house, cars, and bank accounts—splitting the dollar value between us fifty-fifty. Afterward he went through the 401k and the stocks and bonds, which I knew we had. What I did not know was that while my husband was making me go to the church for money, he was saving thousands. When my lawyer was through, he had totaled $800,000 between the two columns. I saw that we could have easily afforded more than $600 for food and gas.

My husband was requiring us to live like paupers while he spent the money in stocks, bonds, rare coins, and alcohol. It was then that I realized we had been living off the money I had made through cleaning toilets and working part-time jobs. Not only was I scrounging for the next dollar to feed my family—I was also going to the church for money when our family did not need it. I was literally taking food out of the mouths of people who truly had nowhere else to turn to but the church. I was devastated to find out how self-centered my husband was. Many would find it odd that I did not know of our financial standing. But what they do not realize is that when you are only allowed to see the taxes each year, it is not enough to go on when you are trying to decipher where money is being spent. When I looked at his W-2 each year with the taxes, the box that was marked for his 401k withholdings had no dollar amount in it, just an X. The 1099 statements were just a tally of gains and losses over the corresponding year, from what I could see. Without being allowed to see the bills or the checking account statements, it was difficult to determine the flow of the money.

It was during this time that I would find out just how manipulative and dishonest my husband truly was. He was trying to regain his security clearance for his government job. Many Department of Energy hearings were scheduled, none of which I was asked to participate in. However, as part of the divorce and custody hearings, I was entitled to a copy of the proceedings of clearance hearings. After much hemming and hawing, my husband and his lawyer provided the transcript to the hearing with all the witnesses' testimony. Reading the hearing transcript was like being transported to a parallel universe where reality was diverted by people covering for a liar. The hearing itself was not designed at getting to the truth; if it had been, qualified witnesses would have been asked to testify. Instead, the hearing was one-sided, geared only at getting my husband in the clear. His lawyer, found at AA, questioned my husband and my husband's list of representatives that included the family therapist who was now his therapist, his brother's, and his boss's. The hearing started with my husband stating he was through with drinking, and he recognized that it was a side effect of being abused by his wife. With the upcoming divorce, he was in charge of his life and emotions, feeling like himself again. The next participant corroborated the story; it was his therapist stating I was the reason my husband drank. She believed the story that I had beaten my husband and then turned to the police to have him removed after I lied about the events. The third witness was his brother who lived in town, the one who was contemplating suicide. He also worked for the government, having the same type of clearance. His statements were more upsetting. He said he hated me from the first day we met. He wished I had never come into the family, and he could not wait until I left.

The last witness was the most devastating to me. It was my husband's supervisor. This man was married to someone who was once my best friend. As a matter of fact, I had introduced them. His statement was, "They should have been divorced long ago." In thinking of that statement, I wondered where he or his wife was when I needed help. Had they ever spoke about me? They were supposedly great Catholics at a sister parish. If he thought we should have been divorced long ago, then at some point he saw the marriage in danger. Where was he then?

What was confusing was that he had seen my husband drink to excess. What did he do as a Christian to assist with the healing of that situation? The hearing went on with the psychologist from my husband's work recommending they check in once a month with each other, then granting my husband his clearance.

Getting his clearance renewed was a doubled-edged sword. My husband was able to continue to pay for Catholic school, so this kept the kids in the stable environment they were used to. However, the clearance also allowed my husband to think he had done nothing wrong. He had sold the idea that I was beating him, and once I was gone, his problems would end. I had to rationalize this decision by remembering my kids were the most important factor, and the lies kept them at a great school.

To not waste any more time while we were waiting for the psychological evaluations to come back in written form, we scheduled a walk-through of the house. This allowed my husband to choose the items he wanted. I had all his clothes packed in suitcases donated by a local shelter, ready for him to take them with him when he left that day. Due to the order of protection, he needed to come with police officers as well as his lawyer. My lawyer was there as well. We all walked through the house as he made his list. Naturally he wanted everything, saying he had owned everything prior to our marriage. He wanted to take all the records when he left, which I refused. He even wanted to go through the garage bolt by bolt, which the lawyers refused. As he was leaving, he took his five suitcases with him. It was around 10:00 a.m. I made a special note of the time because it was his day with the children. He had to pick them up at school in the car line at 3:00 p.m. To have enough room for the kids in the car, he would need to go to his apartment and unload all the suitcases prior to leaving for school.

It was later in the week when I heard from someone who was not very happy with me. She thought I was the most terrible person in the world for sending him with all those suitcases to the car line at school. She felt terrible for him as he cried in the parking lot, not able to get his kids in the car after just being forced out of his home. She took the suitcases with her to store in her garage. I looked her straight in the eye when I said he had left my home at 10:00 a.m., leaving plenty of time to drop the suitcases off at his home. I hoped she could put the pieces together for herself that she had just been manipulated for storage space.

CHAPTER 20

Mediation or Provocation— That Is the Question

Peter wanted to rouse the complacent believers who had listened to the false teachers and believed that because salvation is not based on good deeds they could live any way they wanted. (2 Pt 1:10 NLT)[37]

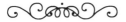

During the next phase of the predivorce proceedings, I learned what mediation was. This was the time that a new lawyer went between the parties getting divorced and stirred up more hurt feelings while each side tried to get what they wanted. This is when I found out my husband was financing his legal fees by using the equity in our home. We owed $7,000 on our home at the start of the divorce; however, he was paying for his side of the divorce as well as his clearance hearing though the home equity line of credit. At the start of mediation, he had converted $40,000 to cash for his lawyer. Apparently, that was illegal, as all of our assets had been frozen the day we started the divorce proceedings. Unfortunately for him, his lawyer did not know this; however, for my side to get the situation rectified, we had to go back to court to obtain an injunction. In addition to the injunction, his lawyer accepted a criminal contempt charge on his behalf. This was a charge that would stay on his permanent record for life. It was then that we realized how inept his lawyer really was. This divorce was more about his lawyer taking him for every dime he could get his hands on.

Had I been a less honest woman, I would have taken their first offer, a fifty-fifty split of finances and time with the children. In retrospect, I would have received a great deal more money, and the time I would have with the children only would have been one night less. However, I was counting on the psychological evaluations to prove that I was the better parent, and my concern was not with the financial standing for my future but the future safety of my children. Although the contempt charge was a win for my side, it started my husband thinking that he was no longer in control. It was not long before my husband fired his alcoholic lawyer and obtained the most expensive divorce lawyer in town. This new lawyer was known as a bully who only cared about winning, not what was best for the children or the truth. He not only knew the divorce laws but he also was as much of a manipulator as my husband. When the psychological evaluations came back in a written report, it was clearly written that I had been abused throughout the marriage. It was also clearly written that I would tell the truth regardless of the consequences. In contrast to my honesty, my husband was diagnosed to be a pathological liar with a drinking problem. The evaluation went on to outline the girlfriend's own issues with losing custody of her children. However, the report stopped short of recommending a custody arrangement and muddied the custody situation further by stating the relationship between my ex and his girlfriend was a "stabling" factor, although it was noted that my husband would drink again. That one comment about seeking stability allowed my husband's new lawyer to twist the facts, social engineering a glorious new life around the bliss of my children with their new mother.

When we met for our second attempt at mediation, we had the evaluator there for clarification. Although the mediator thought this was a great idea, it gave my husband and his lawyer the ability to question the evaluator in hopes of gathering a new way of presenting the facts. The more time they spent with the evaluator, the more questions were asked, and alternate interpretations were created. In the end, although the evaluator was more inclined to view that the long-term care of the children was better off in my hands, he would not put any of his custody recommendations in writing to take to trial. Having just spent almost one year to receive what we had, we could not wait any longer. When we went to our third mediation session, my husband and his lawyer said they found another psychologist to expound on the evaluation, stating that I was unstable. This delighted the mediator because now she had something to focus her negotiations on, as my lawyer explained. This strategy allowed the mediator to sit in my room harping on how they could prove I was an unstable person. She could not divulge any reasoning as to how, just that I was doomed if I proceeded. The truth somehow had been diverted again. During this time, without my knowledge, my husband was passing a petition around the kids' school, at our church, and to our friends asking them to sign if they thought he should be given time with the children. From what I gathered months later, this seemed like a benign petition statement. However, when it was presented in our next mediation session, there was a piece of paper with signatures on it. The statement his lawyer used to present the list of four signatures was that these were the people who stated my husband was the better parent, that I was not in my children's best interest. One of my longtime volunteers had written a letter. Although I was not allowed to read the letter, she later told me that many people have fifty-fifty custody and love it. I asked her if those people have husbands who drive their children drunk and are dating women who have lost custody of their own children. I was polite to her when I said that no one from the outside looking in can offer advice when they only see someone once a week at best. In addition, how could she be a judge when she herself had not lived through what my children were going through? I left her by saying that I realized she was trying her best to understand the situation, but her letter, which was supposed to be to both of us, never came to me. Also, my husband was using it to say that a multitude of people were on his side and said he should have custody. She just looked at me with nothing else to say.

It was time to weigh our options. My lawyer stated this was all "gamesmanship," that it was all part of the procedure. He reminded me that any person could find someone to say whatever they wanted to hear, using the Department of Energy hearing as an example. He stated that paid testimony was a big business. Now it was our turn to go and find another psychologist to say what we wanted them to say. However, I was done with proving that I was not at fault and that my husband was a manipulator. There was just not enough strength left in my soul to handle any more abuse. My lawyer recognized that there was a great deal of pain welling up inside of me. He said, "You just need this to be over, don't you?" I simply nodded. There was nothing left to say. The other side had lied and manipulated so much that I needed to get away from all the negative energy, trading in my sorrows for a lighter load. I accepted a custody split where he had every other week for six days in a row. The children's safety was left to God's hands.

The last two items up for debate were the immense amount of money that had been saved and the personal possessions. One would think that this would be easy. However, his new lawyer had some tricks up his sleeve. My portion of the $800,000 in assets was quickly whittled to a slim $135,000 plus $50,000 of equity in the house. Their rationale was since there was no "comingling" of the investments, I was not entitled to anything else. We argued as to how to divide the rare coin collection and the classic car. We argued on how to divide the artist proofs. We argued on what furniture belonged to whom prior to the marriage. We argued about who would get the furniture in the kids' rooms. In short, we argued.

With everything argued about and the division agreed to, his new lawyer wanted to do another walk through of the house. I refused, knowing that he just wanted to look for new things to argue about. However, my lawyer said it had been a long time since the first walk through, and the judge would grant another since there had been a change in lawyers on his side. I told them I would give them one hour only. I wanted an honest account of the split. I wanted nothing left to chance, no reason left for them to say I was a bad person. Sure enough, it was an expedition to find more to argue about. What they found was a small collection of signed baseballs. What was not listed on the current arrangement stayed in the house, meaning I was keeping the six balls. We used those as leverage to end all the remaining disputes for property. Once all of this was settled and after the closing on the house, it took another six months for him to actually remove the property. It nearly took a court order to have his property removed.

CHAPTER 21

The Day Care

A Prayer for Protection

God, get me out of here, away from this evil;
    protect me from these vicious people.
All they do is think up new ways to be bad;
    they spend their days plotting war games.
They practice the sharp rhetoric of hate and hurt,
    speak venomous words that maim and kill.
God, keep me out of the clutch of these wicked ones,
    protect me from these vicious people;
All boast and swagger, they plot ways to trip me up,
    determined to bring me down.
These crooks invent traps to catch me
    and do their best to incriminate me.
I prayed, "God, you're my God!
    Listen, God! Mercy!
God, my Lord, Strong Savior,
    protect me when the fighting breaks out!
Don't let the wicked have their way, God,
    don't give them an inch!"
These troublemakers all around me—
    let them drown in their own verbal poison.
Let God pile hellfire on them,
    Let him bury them alive in crevasses!

These loudmouths—
don't let them be taken seriously;
These savages—
let the Devil hunt them down!

I know that you, God, are on the side of victims,
that you care for the rights of the poor.
And I know that the righteous personally thank you,
that good people are secure in your presence.
(Ps 140:1–13 MSG)[38]

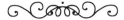

We were done, divorced, and custody was set for life. The girlfriend fully integrated into the kids' lives. The next round of manipulation now began. I was now in charge of stocking both houses with items the kids needed.

It was as if the insignificant property at my home was leaving in backpacks at a slow pace, never to return. Water bottles, lunch coolers, shoes, jackets, sports equipment, and items that I made them when they were small children were disappearing. When questioned about needing the household items, the kids just said they didn't have any at their dad's house. They were told to bring some back.

School uniforms were the fastest-moving items. There was a point where my daughter was borrowing uniforms from children at school because she had only one uniform at my home. She did this without my knowledge; she did not want me upset. But mothers called me looking for their kids' uniforms. When I asked my daughter what was going on, she said all the others were being "held" at her dad's house. It took the counselor getting involved to remedy the disappearance of clothing and household items.

Then there were the homework wars. If homework was forgotten at Dad's, I had to do the retrieving. And of course, the large homework projects could only be completed at my home—I had all the "supplies."

I soon became the task master while the girlfriend became the fun mom. This new mom took the kids on all sorts of adventurous house-hunting expeditions, camping trips with their AA group, and AA-sponsored out-of-state trips to see all the prominent landmarks.

While all this drama was happening at home, school was another matter. The school was being duped into thinking that my ex-husband was the most pleasant man to deal with. He was all smiles and positivity. I was the mean one making everyone toe the line. I wanted to shout at everyone believing him. I wanted to prove him to be what I knew he was—a liar and a cheat. I was angry at everyone falling into his web.

This is when a wise person sat me down and told me it was better to let the events unfold. I needed to change tactics. Eventually he would either reform, or people would see him for what he was.

So that is what I did. I said nothing. I complained about nothing. I kept my mouth shut and prayed for my children's safety.

Within six months, he was drinking so much that his past habits resurfaced. Within eight months, parents at the school were coming up begging me to do something. My ex-husband was showing up at the school totally plastered during my weeks with the kids. But what these people did not realize was that when the kids were in my care, he could drink all he wanted according to the court. His drinking was only an issue when he was responsible for the kids. I informed the multiple people that came to me that they needed treat him just like any other drunk and call 911. The quiet Catholic school had become a comfortable place for him to drink in the parking lot, knowing no one would challenge him.

While the children were in his care, he still drank, but the kids would never confirm or deny it. The people that I knew from school who saw them out never called 911, and one even stated that it should be the kids' responsibility to call. The schoolteachers and parents could now see the light. However, it was still an issue that I was supposed to mysteriously handle as far as they were concerned.

I could not get my children to open up about the drinking. I knew it was an issue, but I did not know how to protect my children. I never saw him drunk when it was his turn to have the kids. When I picked them up, he appeared to be sober, from what I could see from the fifty feet between us. I could not call authorities without seeing him drunk firsthand and the kids, now fourteen and twelve, did not want to report on their dad. With the people we knew from the school not calling 911 when they saw an issue, I did not have recourse to rectify the situation.

One day when it was my turn to pick up the kids at the day care at school, I arrived just as my ex-husband was turning into the parking lot. I had arrived just in time to see my twelve-year-old son get out of the car. When my ex opened his car door, he nearly poured out onto the parking lot. The day-care worker had let my ex get my son and take him out for a smoothie fifteen minutes prior. Here my son had been driving around town with his dad so drunk he could barely form words. I was shocked.

The next day, I went to the principal and told her of the incident. Her comments were that since she did not witness it, I had to be the one to discuss it with the day-care worker. I thought this was odd; however, I went. As I entered the building, I tried to calm myself, knowing that a confrontation would only support my ex-husband's comments that I was intolerable. I asked the director what time my children were picked up, knowing full well that it was fifteen minutes prior to me seeing them in the parking lot. When I described to her what I saw, she would not look me in the eye. I said, "He had to have been in this condition when he entered the building to pick up the kids." Her response was, "I knew he was drunk, but I did not know what to do. I just prayed that God would take care of it." I was stunned. I said that from now on she should call 911 before to the children left with a drunk driver.

The next morning, I wrote a letter detailing the events in a chronological order. I wanted to make sure each statement was a quoted exactly, knowing that there would be another incident. I requested that they provide me with a written plan of action for the future. To make sure that I was not appearing as overbearing, I had a close friend read the letter before I sent it. I left nothing to chance.

Within the week I received a response in writing, stating that they would call 911 in the future. But the procedure was not followed. When I received a phone call the next month from the day care concerning my ex-husband and his sobriety, the 911 procedures were forgotten. He had shown up to pick up the children, and he was turned away due to his incapacitation. It was then that I received a call. I was quite upset when she stated that she sent him off saying, "You need to leave and come back more sober before I can release the children to you." I received a phone call saying she had let him leave alone and she would see how he returned. Within the hour he returned, saying that he prayed and had a cup of coffee. The day-care worker had him walk for her so she could decide if he was able to drive. Then I received the second phone call saying that he was "good enough" to leave with the kids. How prayer and coffee can sober up a person who was walking noticeably impaired just an hour prior I do not know. I was devastated that a day-care professional did not care about the safety of my children.

I took a week to calm down before I addressed the issue. I then wrote a short letter to the principal of the school and the priest of the parish associated with the school. It covered the actual events, plus asked for a written plan of action from the school as to how they planned to rectify this situation. I forwarded this letter plus the previous ones to the bishop of the diocese. Within a week, another letter was sent to me stating that they indeed would call 911. For weeks I prayed to God that someone would be brave enough to call 911 and give me the power I needed to get my children out of this terrible situation. Many came to me stating that they had seen my husband drunk, but no one called 911. On my daughter's fourteenth birthday, I sat in church hiding my tears from her and her friends as I had a long talk with God. I reminded him of the Canaanite story. I stated that I understood he was using our situation to teach others how to stand up for what was right and true. I begged him to stir their hearts faster because my children were in grave danger. I plainly stated that the people witnessing this situation just did not understand the lesson being taught. They did not want to get out of their comfort zone to help others; they did not want their happy life interrupted. They either prayed for God to rectify the situation, or they felt that "someone else" would take care of it. What they did not realize is that God was calling them to action. I felt so defeated, trying to tell God his humans were being human, and he should not expect them to learn a lesson that was beyond their comprehension.

The upcoming week was the week before Christmas. It was my children's time to spend with their dad, as I was to have Christmas night and the week after Christmas. My son was to sing at mass on Saturday night at the parish that I had now joined, the one associated with the school.

I was scheduled to go out of town on business. When I returned home on Saturday night, I had multiple messages on the answering machine concerning mass just two hours before. My ex had shown up intoxicated with the children in tow. Prior to leaving, parishioners those who were not associated with the school called 911, saying he was too intoxicated to drive home. When the police arrived the choir director politely gathered my children, saying she knew me and would get the children to me. With that said, the officer called a cab for my ex and told him to go home. No reports were filed, no breathalyzers taken. I met the director and received a complete verbal account of the incident, and I asked her if she would testify in court and give me the name names of the people who called 911. She stated that she would.

My kids were more terrified than I had ever seen then before. As we pulled up to our home, my ex was waiting in the driveway. I knew better than to stop, so I proceeded to drive around and look at Christmas lights. We called 911 on a cell phone and explained the situation, and they dispatched an officer to remove him from my property. We drove around looking at the lights, and once we noticed my ex's car gone, we went home. Moments later the police were at our door. When I let them in, they said this was their first visit. During their short stay, they informed me that if I could prove that I was keeping the kids from him during his coparenting time as a matter of safety, I would not be sent to jail for contempt of court. They also said to call if he returned.

Shortly after they were gone, the doorbell rang, followed by banging on the door. I went to the door, cracking it just a bit to see my ex-husband. I stated I was keeping the kids because he was drunk, and if he did not leave, I would call the police. He replied that he had not been drinking, he was not arrested, and they did not give him a breathalyzer test. He said I was going to jail for taking his kids without cause. I said "tough" and slammed the door. When I called my lawyer on Monday, his said my job now was to prove people had seen him intoxicated while he had the children so I did not land in jail.

In addition, with it being Christmas the next weekend, I had to find a place where there could be supervised visitation between him and the children or it would appear as if I were being vindictive in the eyes of the court. One week before Christmas—that left me calling all my friends who had said they had seen my ex drinking and asking them to testify in court, finding day care for my son, finding a place for supervised visitation, planning for an extended drive for the holidays, finishing the Christmas shopping, and dealing with the threatening phone calls from ex. I was also working as the only manager on duty for the holidays when our sales numbers were down, and the regional directors were not happy. I was not successful on all fronts. I was able to take care of the immediate needs, travel plans, shopping, visitation, and day care. However, most of my friends were traveling. I had a difficult time linking up with them to discuss what my lawyer needed. In addition, work suffered. How could it not? There was no way to keep all the balls in the air.

Our travel to see grandparents several states away was a relief but bittersweet. I had to find people who had seen my ex drunk with the kids. I was praying that God had stirred people's hearts enough to make them willing enough to get out of their comfort zone, and that my ex had not been sneaky enough to keep the alcohol hidden.

I needed people who could say they saw him drink alcohol without reservation.

Unfortunately, many had seen him drunk, but only one had seen him drink.

My next hurdle was the witnesses to the church event. I needed to obtain the names and phone number of the couple who called 911 for my lawyer. Having never met them, and not even knowing their names, I was at the mercy of the choir director. She had to obtain permission from the priest as well as the couple themselves. It seemed that at every turn there was a roadblock. The Christmas holidays hampered getting in contact with the couple once permission was obtained from the priest to ask the couple if their number could be released. Once the priest's permission was given, the choir director had to ask the couple if they were willing to speak to my lawyer prior to giving me their number. Thankfully, they were willing to be questioned, and the choir director released their contact information to me. After my lawyer spoke to them, he said that they would make wonderful witnesses who didn't know any of us. However, there were some glitches. They had to take care of elderly family members who were sick out of state. But they could testify by telephone if need be. In addition to the one witness who had seen my ex drink with my children present, the couple who called 911 at church, the choir director who was directly involved, and another church employee who witnessed the event, my daughter wanted to testify concerning the evening's events. She was ready to speak for herself about my ex's drinking on that day and others. She finally saw the truth about him. When we returned home, the school allowed me to pick up the kids early each day to prevent any further mishaps with my ex.

When I went back to work after the Christmas holiday, I received a rude awakening. The company I worked for felt that my going through another court battle was not conducive to me working a full-time job. Having been through a divorce with the multiple mediation sessions and interrogatories, the fight for the change in the children's therapist, and the various petitions, my employer knew firsthand how much time I'd be away from office duties. While they had sympathy for my situation and liked me as a person, this was a business decision. As I sat there during the termination meeting, I felt sorry for my supervisor. I could tell it was difficult for her to let me go. I knew she was left with no other options by her superiors. As I drove home, I wondered how I was going to make ends meet in addition tackling the emergency petition to suspend my ex's coparenting time. I filed for food stamps and unemployment compensation the next day.

So there I sat, no job, picking up the kids each day early to prevent another drunk driving incident, and waiting for the court date three weeks later to suspend my ex's coparenting time. I was certain God's plan was about to unfold.

As the court date approached, the human nature of our witnesses began to arise. When it came time to communicate the time and location of the court appearance, the two church employees became hard to reach by phone. I heard through the grapevine that their husbands did not want them involved. To guarantee appearances from all the witnesses, subpoenas were issued. Unfortunately, this required me giving out names and phone numbers without their approval, which caused some animosity. The night before the first court date there was a terrible blizzard, and our court date was postponed another month. When the second date was sent, another round of subpoenas was sent, and everyone was present for court, even the couple who called 911. Looking back, I will always wonder if that snowstorm before the first court date was a gift from God. It gave our star witnesses' family time to heal. When we entered the courtroom, we found that we were thirty-second on the docket, meaning there were thirty-one cases that needed to be heard before ours. That meant that one judge had thirty-two full cases to hear in a six-hour period. Our witnesses, who were already anxious about being there, had to wait a full day in the courthouse with the expectation that our case would not be heard, and they would need to return another day. We went to sit in the courthouse's coffee shop, making small talk to pass the time.

I do not know how the judge accomplished it, but he managed to hear all the cases except ours by 1:30 p.m. When we were ready to proceed into the courtroom, my ex's lawyer stated he would be right back. His reason was he needed to drop something off at another court and would be right back. When forty-five minutes had passed and he was not to be found, the judge informed us that he would wait to hear the case. He also ordered a bailiff to retrieve the attorney. He returned and it was time; we were going to trial. All the witnesses sat outside the courtroom as I and my ex and our lawyers went in and sat across from the judge. This time was different from all the times I had been in this court room. This time there was only us there; usually it was filled with people waiting to be heard. The room was usually hot, crammed with people whispering amongst themselves. You could barely hear what was happening at the front with the judge. Now it was silent and cold. Any movement and sound echoed within the bare room.

When both sides presented their case, I found out something interesting. My ex had had another psychological evaluation by an alcohol counselor. The test confirmed that he was an alcoholic and recommended a specialized counselor. This may sound odd, but I rejoiced. Now he could no longer deny that he had a drinking problem. It seemed like a hollow victory when moments later the judge stated he was stepping out for five minutes to allow us to come to a resolution amongst ourselves. No resolution could be made, and all our witnesses came to speak, including my daughter. I wanted them heard. I also wanted supervised visitation, something that my ex would not approve. When the judge returned, he had all the witnesses come into the court room to hear his statement and the proceedings. He thanked them for coming but said he recognized there was a drinking problem and did not need them to testify. He went on to say that my ex could have full visitation rights if he went to an alcoholic rehabilitation counselor while wearing an alcohol detection bracelet around his ankle. The bracelet was the kind that detected alcohol from the normal sweat on the skin. Once that was in place, the kids were to return to their normal coparenting schedule.

So, there it was—the verdict. I lost my job, the kids were terrified, and the witnesses were stressed out from being involved. All of this to get an ankle bracelet on a man who swore he did not have a drinking problem. The school had been patiently waiting for an outcome that would get them away from any liability that stemmed from surrendering children to a drunk driver. However, all I could give them was a notice that my ex was wearing a bracelet that would monitor if he was drinking. The school would still have to rely on physical cues to determine whether he was sober when the kids were getting in the car. Over the next three weeks, the kids' fear subsided, and they decided they did not want to change the custody arrangement at all. Over the next three months my ex did not drink, or he rigged the bracelet not to detect if he did drink.

CHAPTER 22

I Want to Be a Nun
for Halloween

God may have seemed slow to these believers as they faced persecution every day and longed to be delivered. But God is not slow; he just is not on our timetable. Jesus is waiting so that more sinners will repent and turn to him.

We must not sit and wait for Christ to return, but we should live with the realization that time is short and that we have important work to do. Be ready to meet Christ any time, even today; yet plan your course of service as though he may not return for many years. (2 Pt 3:8–9 NLT)[39]

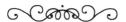

Another year had passed. Dealing with the day-to-day movement of the kids' belongings and the kids themselves kept my mind full. Job hunting was rough. I had started my own cleaning business, something I had done prior to being married and having children. It was just to make ends meet, and it was cash under the table. Between child support, unemployment, and cleaning I was financially fine, but unemployment was coming to an end.

It was my turn to have the kids for Christmas Eve and Christmas morning this year. With my son in the choir at my church, we needed to be there early and sit in the balcony. Finding our way to the very front balcony pew, I sat on the aisle with my daughter to my right. There was not much room in the pew, so I sat kind on a weird angle. My feet were smashed between the step, a speaker, and the balcony wall. There was not an inch to spare. Every time someone wanted out of the pew, I had to stand and move up the steps for them to get out.

Although my ex had told my son he would be going to his own parish, he showed up intoxicated at ours. How he managed to get from one place to another in his condition, I will never know. He was an usher at his parish, so when he arrived, he began ushering. He stumbled through the center aisle, even though this was not his parish. He shook hands with many people, and at some point, someone must have asked him to sit down because they did not need help ushering.

When the singing began, he came to the balcony, proceeding to make himself visible to those around him. He shook hands with every person on the ends of the aisles as he found his way to the pew directly two rows behind me and my daughter.

Regardless of the restraining order, there he was.

I am not saying that he caused a scene; he acted more like someone who is going out of his way to be noticed for being a good Christian. He prayed loudly, sang at the top of his lungs, and spoke to everyone around him even though there were times we were supposed to be quiet. His behavior did not go unnoticed. During mass, an acquaintance of mine who was sitting in the pew behind me leaned over and asked me if he was drunk. I just nodded. What was I going to do? Have a conversation?

During communion, he came down to the edge of the balcony to look over. He literally was standing on my feet as he looked over the rail. So much was going through my head. I could not scream out in pain; we were in church. I could not move; he would have flipped over the side. I could not tell him to move; he would have caused a bigger scene. If he had fallen, with my luck I would have been charged with murder on Christmas Eve. He ignored us, although we were within inches of each other.

Thankfully he wandered back to his seat before we had to get up for Communion. I limped to the Communion station and back to my seat without incident. After mass, people gave me their sympathies as we waited for the church to empty. We were the very last to leave to ensure that he would not be around. We ran to the car quickly. I felt silly, but who wants to be in a confrontation on Christmas Eve?

After Christmas break, my son was asked to play Daddy Warbucks in the school's production of *Annie*. There was a great deal to be done. Plenty of lines to memorize and songs to learn. This was a big deal. This would be my son's first time starring in a school play, and he was in seventh grade.

There were countless late-night practices, and my son was a bit nervous having to sing a solo in front of a large group. When the big night came, he put on his bald cap and was ready for the show. My husband and I agreed that we would both go to the Friday show as that was my son's only performance. I reminded my husband about the restraining order and to stay away from me. However, that fell on deaf ears. He sat two rows behind me, drunk. Before the curtain opened, I found a teacher and reported the issue. I did not want my son embarrassed by his dad being loud or falling out of the chair. She had the gall to say that she was being a parent that night and would not get involved. So, I found another teacher, and her husband was a policeman in another city. He corralled my husband and took him outside with stern warning not to come back inside.

The play went off without a hitch.

As we were putting chairs away and waiting for the kids to change, I saw the principal. I went over to tell her of the events before the play. I was disgusted with the way the first teacher acted. So there I went, telling her all the details. Did I get an "I'm sorry"? No. Her statement was, "He can be drunk on school property!"

Yes, those exact words came out of her Catholic mouth.

I was livid. With all the documentation of the lack of concern, she said *that*. I lost it. I looked her straight in the eye and said, "Do you realize that I have enough documentation to sue you? Personally? For dependency neglect? I won't sue the church or the school. This is your doing. And since, as a nun, you only own three sets of habits, get ready to run this school naked! I will sue you for all three!"

Her mouth hung open. I turned and left, calling my lawyer as I gathered my two kids. I had to leave a voice mail, which was a good thing because I was mad.

My lawyer called me on the next day, and when I explained what I wanted, he burst out laughing. He could not believe I was serious. I finally convinced him that I wanted all her clothing because that was all that she owned. He asked why suing the church or school would not work. When I answered that they hide behind ignorance, stating they told her to do her job, he agreed to write a threatening letter, but no more. He said he just could not sue a nun; he was an Episcopalian.

When his letter was received, we got a follow-up letter from the bishop, the priest, and the principal expressing their deepest regret and saying it would never happen again.

But it did happen. Over and over. There was nothing that I could do. No one would confront my husband, and no one would call 911. I was told that if I called 911, I would suffer in the court system by looking like a bully.

To make it through the day, I had to get some perspective on this situation. It occurred to me that God does not want anyone destroyed by his pain. He wants everyone to learn and to be given every opportunity to change. God used the Christmas Eve mass and the spring play to allow everyone to learn what he or she needed to practice on. With these situations, one sin of commission on a true sinner's part was instigating a multitude of sins of omission. Over time, I knew my children's and my persecution would be eliminated, but not in my time. My children and I are just part of God's plan to save us all.

I had no full-time job; I worked several part-time teaching jobs to make ends meet. By this point, my husband's judgment with drinking and driving the children from school had been well documented. I had spoken to the principal, Sister Anne Katherine, multiple times about my husband's flagrant intoxication on the school property. I had written letters to her about the laxness of the day care. When I received no response, I wrote the priests in charge of the of the parish that the school was associated with. I had gone so far as to write the bishop after receiving no help from the priests and the principal. No one would help me get the kids out of that terrible situation. I was back to just praying that someone would call 911 while he was drunk with the kids so my ex's influence in their lives would be limited.

CHAPTER 23

Sins of Commission and Omission

God has given each of you a gift from his great variety of spiritual gifts. Use them well to serve one another. Do you have the gift of speaking? Then speak as though God himself were speaking through you. Do you have the gift of helping others? Do it with all the strength and energy that God supplies. Then everything you do will bring glory to God through Jesus Christ. All glory and power to him forever and ever! Amen. (1 Pt 4:10–11 NLT)[40]

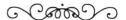

Everyone has a special gift and usually more than one. One of my gifts is endurance. Many people (including priests) have told me I am unwavering when I am in a situation and I know that what I am doing is right and just. I take the teachings of sins of commission and omission to heart. But this gift has brought me a great deal of suffering.

God uses suffering. One possible way he does this is by trying to teach his followers to analyze situations before rushing in. Sometimes we may take over someone else's problems when they are suffering. Here they have their own talent that God is trying to get them to use.

God trying to get us to use our own talents that he gave us and let others use the talents that he gave them.

Because of my ability to endure, I used to take on the pain of others while dealing with my own pain. I would do this by accepting projects and problems that no one else wanted. I felt this problem needed to get dealt with, and because my gift was fixing problems, I should be the one to muddle through it. Sometimes I even relished the thought of succeeding in these difficult tasks.

However, as time progressed, I came to realize that taking on problems that no one wanted to deal with prevents others from growing. I realized over time that when we accept other's problems, we undo God's plan by not letting the right person learn from the suffering associated with his plan as it unfolds.

Another concept that I learned over time was when a painful experience or difficult season comes our way and situation is truly ours to experience, we should not view it as a punishment. We should look on this difficult time as a teaching moment from God. As children of God, we need to switch our thinking about painful situations. We need to think of them as a holistic learning process.

By being holistic, we first recognize God loves us enough to try to take us to the next level of faith in Him. It then becomes possible to see that God trusts us to deal with this new period of strife in a Christian manner. If we stay focused on the positive aspects of pain leading to personal growth, we can stretch our minds to believe that God might be using us as a teaching moment for others. It just might be possible that our personal suffering that is not caused by our own negligence is for the glory of God. When looking at painful times in this manner, we can see how God uses secondary circumstances to shake up complacent believers. God uses pain in many ways and always for his glory.

God puts people in situations to see how they will handle them. But I believe that God also wants to see how people react to someone else's suffering. I bet he is trying to determine whether people will follow The Ten Commandments.

Here, people are dealing with a true sinner and the circumstances are beyond their control. The question is "Will the community viewing this type of pain stay in their comfort zone and avoid getting involved?" Maybe in these types of situations, God is trying to determine whether people will use the talent he has given to them to help those in need. Here, if we ignore the problem, we accept the sin being created within the situation as our own. In this setup, it is possible that God is trying to determine whether people will commit sins of commission and omission.

God wants to see his people perform the good deeds—the ushering, prayer, giving money, singing in the choir, setting up chairs. etc. These are active works done in his name. But we should remember that God also works in secondary circumstances to teach us as well as judge us. Are we ignoring difficult situations because they take us out of our planned schedule? Have we walked away from a painful quick task that came out of the blue thinking, *Someone else can handle that?* God wants to see us actively work in the fun events that make us sweat together. This builds a community. However, I feel God is more impressed with the painful, quiet acts that we perform when no one is watching. The quiet, painful acts of mercy show that we care about our community.

When we can look at our neighbor's suffering as a teaching moment for us, then we begin to understand God's plan for pain. We begin to truly address sins of commission and omission. Many will scoff at this thought process; however, I firmly believe that we rack up more sins of omission than we care to admit. We must remember that the line that separates right from wrong, or good from evil, runs through us from our brain to our heart. Sins of commission are easy to avoid if we use our brains. However, sins of omission take a more heartfelt approach. When we try to stay on the right side of the line, the line becomes blurred, causing us to choose between what we want to do and what we want to avoid.

There is one thing that must not be forgotten. A thousand years is like a day to God, so he isn't really being slow about answering us, as some people think. No, he is being patient for our sake. He does not want anyone to be destroyed but wants everyone to repent.

CHAPTER 24

Stumbling Block Progress

God had opened my eyes to my blindness. I no longer believed that people I loved would never be dishonest. I just did not know how to handle it. I still became angry with people who were straight-up lying. I stopped short of asking myself the tough questions of why they were lying. I was just mad.

Anger was still my go-to emotion. Anger at myself. Anger at my husband for being a drunk. Anger at my family for not helping. Angry at my husband's family for continuing to ignore the problem, and anger at the people around me from the church and school for not getting involved. My anger level had not changed.

My anger stemmed from my impatience. When I began to have the heart-to-heart conversations with God, I was still not prepared for a time lag. I was not patient and could not see or hear God's answer. My family came first to me, not God's family. I was impatient that God was using my family so his family could witness the disaster. I did not want to be an example for God's family of losers. They were not paying attention. They were not getting the point. And we were suffering.

I had regained my self-esteem, but to the point that I was arrogant. My suffering made me feel entitled, and we all know that pride goes before the fall. I still did not have the ability to examine my thoughts against what was appropriate for the situation. My thoughts, and consequently my actions, were a big stumbling block for me.

My worldly strength was in all its glory. *I was not* examining my soul. *I was* going to turn this ship around and God *was* going to help me do it. *I was* tearing my stumbling block *down.*

Do you think that worked? I was, again, too capable for my own good, which led to having no boundaries. Plus, no one wanted to help a bully butting in everywhere. And God let me learn my lessons.

THE
RETRIBUTION

CHAPTER 25

Fear of Choosing When I Was Young and Where That Has Left Me Now

When God opens a door it's for our provision, when he keeps it closed it is for our protection. Our Past presents our Future. Read your life backwards. What you have done, or failed to do, opens or closes doors for your future. You can miss God's Provision and Protection if you are not paying attention. God's Provision and Protection are not what we expect—His plan is different than our own.[41]
—Max Lucado

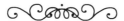

Finding full-time employment and being able to afford home repair became major issues. I knew that teaching part time was not a long-term solution; however, I had hoped it would turn into a full-time job. I taught a class or two each semester. I rotated between three different colleges depending on the need. I mostly taught at night or on Saturday mornings when the kids were young, so a sitter was not needed. When they started school, I also picked up a couple of day classes. The upside was I was building a great resume; the downside was I taught at colleges that were sometimes an hour away. With travel expenses I did not make much, but over time I could choose campuses that were closer to home. When I had several classes during each semester, everything seemed to be in place. I could still take care of the kids, volunteer at the school, and hold several different volunteer positions at the church. I had enough money to take care of household expenses as well as pay for activities for the kids. I spent all my income on the kids or the house, saving nothing. It was easier than fighting with my husband. I took on more cleaning jobs from time to time when I ran a little short.

I had high hopes that I would land a permanent position at one of the three colleges that I rotated between. Teaching at the college level had always been a lifetime dream of mine. When an opening came at one of them, I put in my application right away. It was then that I learned that the degree I held was too specialized to be useful. According to the accrediting board, my degree did not contain the coursework with the prefixes that would allow me to teach the classes I was currently teaching. My prefixes were from a sister discipline; however, there was a big accrediting push to eliminate instructors who were teaching out of discipline. I was distraught.

I revamped my resume into several different versions, applying for everything that came open in industry. I exercised all my contacts, having them hand deliver resumes and cover letters. This allowed me to apply to most of the major employers throughout the city. I was still teaching at this time, and it looked like a position was opening at the college I wanted to stay with. I remember sitting on the ground at a college festival praying feverishly that I would be interviewed. I was teaching four classes for them at the time, and the position focused on volunteering for the community. In addition, they had a professor who held the same degree as mine. All indications from the staff and the students looked like my search would be over, and I would be chosen. Unfortunately, all my planning and praying did not pay off. I was not even on the interview list.

No one would give an explanation as to why; however, I surmised it was due to an issue in one of my night classes that had presented itself at the same time as the position opened. One of the female students found out that we had a registered sexual predator in our class. With security being scarce at night, she was concerned about walking to her car. I tried my best to keep her and the entire class of women safe by asking my lead instructor what to do. He just happened to be the hiring professor as well. He had no recommendations, other than to alert Student Affairs, which I did. Nothing happened; there was no security in the parking lot when we left at night. We were the only class getting out at night from that building, and nothing was done to promote safety. This annoyed me, but there really was not much more I could do. However, in retrospect, it appeared to me that just by asking for assistance, I was labeled a boat-rocker or a rogue instructor who would eventually get the school sued. By looking out for someone else, I failed to look out for myself.

I never taught for that school again. What's worse, there was one more college that had a full-time position. That last college interviewed me for an open position, and I came in as their second choice. My life's goal was over. There were no more options. I blamed God. I was good enough to teach Sunday school, but not good enough to have a full-time job that would allow me to be self-supporting. I had a sinking suspicion that God wanted to keep me in the situation I was in—doing his work with no regard for my welfare.

In addition, the resumes that I was sending out to the employers around town did not net me very many interviews. The personal references from my high-powered MBA students did not help much either. Life could not get much bleaker. I was now completely jobless, and my ex-husband did not attempt sobriety. This is when I began to examine my past to figure out how I came to be in such a terrible mess.

I looked back on how I chose my college degree, since the type of degree seemed to be my current problem with finding a job. I remember in college being very concerned about being in my sophomore year without a clear major. I had taken an accounting class, which was quite easy. I was unclear why everyone was stressed about it. I also took a computer programming course with the same level of ease. However, I had no clue what career path would result from these. I had no one at home to ask and felt ill-prepared to ask instructors. I stood in the middle of the library complex and said to myself, *I should just stick to what I know, something will come of that.* Unfortunately, what I knew was how to sew and how to organize a sales floor. So I took more classes centered on those topics, planning to get a master's degree to teach college in the same discipline. I made the decision out of fear. I decided on my career by taking the path of least resistance, because I was afraid of trying something new.

When I was studying for my master's degree, I had the opportunity to change colleges to the more prestigious and versatile MBA program. However, I chose not to because I was afraid of not having a teaching assistantship to pay for it. When I received an internship, which allowed me to live on campus and take as many classes as I wanted to, I still did not switch to the program that was better for the long term. I was shortsighted, and I used an ill-formed decision-making process that led to poor educational choices. My poor choices, made because of fear, led me to poor career opportunities. It was then that I realized that God had tried to provide for me early on, but I was not paying attention.

When I looked at my marriage, I suddenly felt the same way. There were plenty of times my husband had shown his true feelings toward me. However, I rationalized them away when I should have taken them as a sign of times to come. Was it possible that God was trying to protect me from ending up in the current situation I was in? If so, why couldn't I find a job to get me out of the situation? Where were his provisions now?

Missing God's provisions was a hard pill to swallow. When I look at my life in reverse order, I can easily see key moments where decisions changed my options. Even if God had tried to show me that my husband's behavior would never change, I still could not believe that God would want me to leave a man who at one time had been so good. He used to be my best friend, truly honest and thoughtful when we first met. I had to believe it was the alcohol that caused him to change, and, like the fertility problems, God would see us through to the other side as a family.

It was just a stumbling block we needed to get through.

CHAPTER 26

My Daughter Leaving

Being a good parent is knowing when not to do
something for your children.
—Rick Chinn

God loves you enough to strip away anything
that gets between his relationship with you. God
made his purpose clear. He is not interested in our
having a good life. He is interested in an intimate
relationship with us. He is interested in our spiritual
transformation. It is in the middle of crisis that we
are ready to listen to Him.[42]
—Pete Wilson

The truly religious believe that God can do anything, and he can.
But what happens when you are off God's intended path for you? What
happens when you let someone or something come between you and
your relationship with God? God must get you back on track in some
way. One year had passed, and we were still having some of the same
problems with my ex, but much progress had been made as well. The
teachers at my son's school acknowledged the need for caution for my
son. My close friends realized that even though it may be difficult,

sometimes speaking up is what God is calling us to do. Although these may be small miracles, I am happy for the progress.

My son, now thirteen, and my daughter, now fifteen, were going back and forth between the two houses. My daughter was in high school and was getting unhappier with each trip to her dad's. I thought: *She has been putting up with this all her life.*

I remember once we were all reading downstairs. It was right after our daughter learned to walk. My husband was reading the Sunday paper, and I was reading books to my daughter. She would walk one over, I would read it to her, and then she would take it back, tottering along. For some unknown reason, my husband picked her up and walked upstairs. He did not say a word. He just walked up the stairs, and then he locked the door, leaving me locked downstairs. I thought it was a mistake, so I banged and banged on the door. I went outside through the garage and rang the doorbell. He never came. After forty-five minutes, I called his mother in Kentucky. I told her what happened, and I asked her to call her son and tell him to let me upstairs to be with my child. When she did, my husband immediately unlocked the door. However, afterward he made me call his mother and apologize for involving her in our fight. I explained to her that I did not know we were fighting, but she was convinced otherwise. To this day I do not remember even having an ill word with my husband.

I should have recognized then that something was not kosher, but who would go around inventing conversations that had not taken place? At that time, I loved this man; he was the smartest person I had ever met. He was fun and loved kids as well as the elderly. He never met a stranger, and he had a clear plan for his life. Why on earth would he invent stories?

The manipulative behavior of my husband was so covert in the beginning. He started internal chaos within me, something inside of me that I could easily see but that I doubted was true. It was like déjà vu. I knew something was wrong; however, it always appeared to be me or something I caused. My husband's depictions of events were so smoothly put together that no one could tell he was lying. For years, my husband would twist events to present me as less than desirable. I had either made a wrong choice that resulted in our family demise, or I was somehow the root of all evil. He had a way of belittling and demeaning that I had never been exposed to. He made backhanded compliments and would state an opinion only to totally deny it later.

When I think of the times I took him at face value and went to bat for him, only to find out he lied, I am ashamed of myself. There have been several times when I pitched fits to get what my husband said needed to be corrected because he was wronged. Later, I would find out what the true circumstance was, and he would say, "You must have misunderstood me, but you were doing so well at getting things taken care of that I did not want to correct you."

Now my fifteen-year-old daughter was receiving this same treatment, and she would not talk about it.

My daughter kept busy with sports and studying. She stayed in her room at my place, and I did not press her for information. But I knew.

My daughter's schedule was intense. She was an honor student who was heavily involved in school clubs. She was my overachiever. Mixing all her activities with the psychologist's appointments was like a Tetris game, but it worked. She found rides to events at the high school while I ferried her brother back and forth to middle school.

While at her dad's, my daughter dealt with the scheduling and the mind games. And then my daughter had enough.

It was my ex's week, and I heard the door rattle. When I got to the door it opened and she came through it in a heap. In a bundle of hurt and tears, she began to tell her story. It was the same as mine, word for word. She asked me how I put up with it for so long. When I said, "I had two good reasons that I loved," she cried even harder. And then she paused and in a breathy voice she said, "I left my brother over there."

I just held her tighter and said that I bet God had a plan, and she did not need to go back.

CHAPTER 27

911

The good man is the man who no matter how morally
unworthy he has been is trying to become better.
—Unknown

Forgiving is not forgetting; it is letting go of the hurt.[43]
—Mary McLeod Bethune

So there we were, my daughter living with me full time and going
to all of the high school events she could cram into a day, and my
son splitting his time between his dad and me. My son was a gentle
scholar, not a sportsman. His favorite sport was a reading a book, and
he loved chemistry. By dropping his bookbag at the end of his bed, he
was able to cocoon himself into a world where only he existed. This
behavior left him alone at his dad's, but relatively unchallenged.

But there was a downside to this.

Not confronting my ex-husband about his drinking gave that man
the feeling that it was OK to drink whenever he wanted. And once
he started, there was no stopping until he passed out. With years
of drinking experience, it took a great deal of alcohol to make that
happen. He could drink a fifth of whiskey and still talk without a
slur. He had become the hardest alcoholic to contend with—a highly
functional drunk. He went to work in the morning, drinking and

driving. He drank on the way home, drinking and driving. I can only assume he drank while he was at work too. Between the Halls cough drops and being able to speak clearly, no one could tell when he was drinking and when he wasn't. And by the end of the day, he just crawled into the bottle until he passed out.

My thirteen-year-old son was caught between getting what he needed and living in his own bubble. He chose the bubble. He didn't keep track of anything while at his dad's. His homework, his laundry, and his bathroom routine were all up for grabs. Sometimes they would get done, and sometimes they wouldn't. This meant that sometimes he went to school clean, and sometimes he didn't. And the small Catholic school did not question his appearance. You can only guess as to how bad it got with the school not calling me about it and me not seeing him for a week. The court-appointed counselor tried to help, but my son just retreated into his bubble.

Then there were the trips around town with dad. My ex had gotten comfortable. No one wanted to confront him about his drinking. He was a mean man. So he drank while he was driving. He drank in parking lots while he was waiting for my son to get out of school functions. He drank inside places he and my son would go—the museum, the church, the grocery store, you name it. But since he was highly functional and could walk a straight line while talking normally, people said he wasn't drunk.

As my ex-husband became more comfortable, the stories began to flood in. "I saw your poor son at (fill in the blank)." And where was dad? Off somewhere drinking, I am sure.

But you cannot fix what you cannot prove.

I remembered I told my daughter that God would have a plan to help my son get away from his father for good. I could not pray loud enough for that plan to get started. What I did not realize was it was already started and going full steam ahead. God was waking my son up as gently as he could.

I had to practice being a patient warrior again, waiting for God to build up to the crescendo. One block at a time, God was building

it. I had been here before—no one calling 911, no one helping my
children, no one taking ownership. But as a great spiritual writer, Pete
Wilson, once wrote:

> God has a great deal of power. To witness it you must
> first take the spiritual risk of trusting him. God's
> power is released when someone trusts him enough
> to obey. For faith to work we have to move before,
> we are sure.[44]

I was faithful; I trusted God would do something. I kept placing
my son in his father's hands not knowing how bad the drinking was.
Then I prayed and waited on my Heavenly Father for the answer.

My son ended up going to jail with his father three times between
seventh grade and before he entered high school. Thankfully, my son
ended up in the lobby waiting to be picked up. After each event, I
traipsed down to court for a change in custody. But each time my ex
was awarded with an alcohol monitoring bracelet, and our custody
arrangement went back to the way it had been. What was the court's
thinking? That it was only public intoxication, he was not driving? My
son was in no danger?

Every time that ankle monitoring bracelet went on, it stayed on a
little longer. The judge thought he could find the breaking point for
my ex. The point where he would wise up and stay sober. That judge
was more interested in seeing my ex as a victim than an abuser. He did
not care about any mental damage my son was suffering, only that my
son didn't look harmed.

At the start of my son's freshman year at high school, God
finally answered. It was my ex-husband's weekend and, true to
form, there was always a drink in his hand. This just happened to
be a weekend with a very large two-part event in the downtown
area that my son was a part of. My ex dropped off my son at the first
part and went on to places unknown. When the event was over, my
son could not find him to take him to the rest of the event, which

required getting back to his high school. My son called me, and I was thirty minutes away.

I started out, and at the halfway point I got another call. It was my son again. He called to say his dad had showed up and not to worry.

What? Don't worry? I told him not to get in the car. I knew what state he was in. But my son, thinking only that he was late, said he had to go.

Click.

Now what? I was driving toward *what*? What should I do? Stop? Turn around and go about my day? Continue and find my son? Go to the venue and make sure he was okay?

I could not think for the fear running through my mind. Then the phone rang again. It was 911. She made me pull over before she would talk to me.

The pit in my stomach was about to burst.

I could barely get the words "I am parked" out as I was choking back the tears. My mind went to the worst possible situation, a severe car accident. However, I was wrong. God had been putting building blocks in my son's mind, and they finally clicked. He realized what kind of danger he was in, and he called 911 on his dad.

The 911 operator was calling to tell me that they had pulled him over for drunk driving and child endangerment. I needed to come for my son, who was safe inside a grocery store. My tears became tears of joy. I thanked her a thousand times and drove like the wind.

When I pulled up my son was giving his statement to the police. He looked so grown up. He was no longer the little man I needed to protect. He was a man who could take care of himself. And where was his father? Handcuffed in the backseat of the police car. I looked at him only to see a shadow of a man that I once knew. Unshaven and slumped over, his hair needed to be cut and washed. His clothes were mismatched and rumpled. This was a man who used to write computer programs for government agencies.

When my son was through with his statement, we continued to his event. I called his counselor to update her on the police events, and to my surprise, she wrote protection orders that prohibited my ex from communicating with the children until they were eighteen.

God had worked his magic and put us under his protective wings for a period. We were safe, free from alcoholic drama for a few years. We were normal for two years, and it was bliss.

CHAPTER 28

My Daughter Turning Eighteen

For the LORD sees clearly what a man does, examining every path he takes. An evil man is held captive by his own sins; they are ropes that catch and hold him. He will die for lack of self-control; he will be lost because of his great foolishness. (Prv 5:21–23)[45]

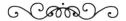

On my daughter's eighteenth birthday my ex could begin to communicate with her again. Have you ever met someone obsessed with getting something done? That was my ex on my daughter's eighteenth birthday. If he thought of something, he emailed her asking for an answer. He wanted to have that answer right away, so he would email again, and again ... and again.

And again.

For that one question he might email her five or six times, and there were seven or eight questions like that a day. Every day. My daughter handled it all professionally, like a secretary. She blocked off a section of time to deal with "dad emails." When that time was up, she left the remaining emails for the next day. She was very professional. No emotion on the outside. Inside, I was unsure of how she felt. She had learned that if she expressed it to me, I would go bonkers and take legal action. So she motored on, veiled in professionalism.

She was involved in every event imaginable at school, and she excelled as an honor student. Her dad never came to the high school, though. It was a large public school, with police security. But he did make it to every church event my daughter attended. If she was reading at mass, he was there to watch. Any holiday, he was there. Just a regular church service, he was there. It was like he was her own private paparazzi. He was the disheveled drunk old man who stumbled around mooning after her. I did not know what to do. This is where my kids graduated middle school. This where their roots were. I did not want to leave.

When I asked my daughter how she felt, she said she felt sad for him. She said this was the only way he could see her, and that at least he wanted to see her. She told me to leave things alone.

So I did. And for a time, it worked.

Their dad could see the children at church, but at school, a public school where there was a police presence, he was nowhere to be found. My kids discussed their thoughts with a counselor, and I job hunted and volunteered at the church and the school. As for my ex, he drove around drinking as he waited for Sundays to come.

He found another high-powered job but lost it. He went to a mixer that served alcohol and drank until he passed out. On another occasion he walked to lunch, and on his way back, he was arrested for drunk and disorderly conduct.

My kids had nothing to do with this nonsense. My ex's behavior was winning him bad behavior awards, and we had to do nothing. The day had come where people were getting involved, and we didn't have to do anything! Yes, it was sad. For people looking in at our pain, it had to be sad. For those families who lived in that small Catholic parish, and had seen everything evolve over the years, it was epic. It had to be a reminder of the tragedy of what could have been.

It was around Christmas when the parish celebrated the graduating seniors and my daughter was asked to give a reading at mass. Of course, I sat front and center. Where was her father? The front row of the balcony, so she could see him and know he was there.

How this did not unnerve her while reading to a full church I will never know. I was just sitting there, and it made my skin crawl. But she just read her passages and sat down.

Afterward, a few people came up to me and expressed their sorrow on how our lives had turned out. "Your broken family was so awful to look at," one parishioner stated. He went on to say, "I remember when your family was young; it was picture-perfect, so beautiful. It was so hard to look at you now."

I could not help thinking *Where were you when I asked for help to keep my beautiful family together?* You were busy. You could not be bothered. Now you find it hard to look at the results. What do you want me to say to you? I struggled to put food on the table and keep my kids on the straight and narrow. And you find it hard to look at us.

What do you want me to say to you?

I smiled, nodded, and waved at a nonexistent person behind him. I was shaking inside. I was clenching my teeth; I was looking for my kids so we could go. I wanted to be done.

I gathered my kids and left. We returned to the safety of our home and shut out the world. My son to his books. My daughter to her projects. And me to the TV remote. Just nothingness. Quiet nothingness for the rest of the day. I knew, come the next day, Monday, I had another legal battle.

When my daughter turned eighteen, it was her senior year in high school. The protection order was removed for her, but my husband still had to pay child support. This was a fact that confused him, so I found myself taking him to court one more time.

CHAPTER 29

A Shell of a Man

What are worthless and wicked people like? They are constant liars, signaling their deceit with a wink of the eye, a nudge of the foot, or the wiggle of fingers. Their perverted hearts plot evil, and they constantly stir up trouble. But they will be destroyed suddenly, broken in an instant beyond all hope of healing. (Prv 6:12–15)[46]

Satan wears many faces throughout the Bible. Those faces, much like human faces, do not reveal his true intentions. He uses his faces to misrepresent the truth and to turn as many people as he can away from God. Satan wants us to not feel guilty for deceiving others. When we stop feeling guilty for sin, our soul is dead. He is, of course, the father of all lies. And where else to sort out the truth but the courtroom?

So, there we were, at the courthouse one more time. I came to get the truth straight, one more time. I had my lawyer and all his files, and my ex had his lawyer. We had an afternoon time slot. I came prepared with a book and a bottle of water, finding a spot to sit for a long afternoon of waiting. Court time never was accurate.

One thing about going to court is there is a great deal to entertain you in the waiting room. Watching people come in and out of the different chambers held my interest. There were all sorts on their worst days. Satan was ever present here.

As the day wore on, the antechamber emptied. My lawyer was busy handling his other cases, as was my ex's lawyer. I read my book and watched people file in and out of the judges' chambers. We were no better or no worse than any other couple trying to get their lives separated from each other. There was no line for white-collar and blue-collar people. There were just people. Some crying, some staring straight ahead like me. All of us waited for the inevitable, our turn to find out if we were to be believed.

My ex was wearing the face of a concerned friend for every victim wanting to be heard. He trolled the antechamber like a miner looking for a nugget of gold. He sat and listened to whomever wanted to divulge their story. He consoled them with a shoulder to cry on and a warm hug as they left to find out their fate.

As I sat and watched this spectacle, I thought, *The judge cannot see you here, who is this show for?* I knew this concern for people he did not know was not real. Was this part of his legal scheme? To have this concern on closed-circuit TV to show that he was a caring individual? My mind rolled this newfound source of information round in my head. How could he possible use the stories of others in our court battle?

Once again, we were the last case to be heard. The antechamber emptied except for my ex, me, and my lawyer's belongings. I took the time to use the ladies' room. The lawyers were in with the judge, so we were next. When I came back through the door I was stunned.

There was my ex going through my lawyer's papers. But that was not the scary part. When my ex glanced up at me by chance, I did not see his face.

What did I see?

I saw a black masked image, like the frowning imaged you see at Mardi Gras. My ex was not wearing a mask; *his face was the mask.* And when he looked at me in the face, I was frozen in the door frame. I could not move or speak. And what was worse, I wet myself, even though I had just emptied my bladder.

This black masked image was there for a second. But I knew I had just seen the devil. When it was gone, I could move again, but I stood in the door frame, shaking. My ex put the top back on the box and scurried to a part of the room where I could not see him. I went back into the bathroom and cleaned up as best I could before we were called in.

I was still shaking when we were in the courtroom. I was not listening to the judge. I could not believe what I saw, but what other explanation was there? I thought, *Was this is all the reason for the bravado, the showmanship, and the confidence?* He is relying on the father of lies who was living inside of him.

A great calm came over me. I remembered lies never win in the end. I play the long game. I have the truth. I have God. I tried to settle myself and concentrate on the proceedings before me.

At that point in time, I had not really looked at my ex in a long time. Yes, I had seen him, but I had not actually taken stock of how he had changed in appearance. I really had not noticed. My mind kept wandering back to black image. I wanted to *know* what it was, what happened, and if I was irrational.

It was then that I stole a glance at my ex. It was the last time I saw him alive. He appeared pale. His blue eyes seemed to be looking out into the distance, not focused on anything. It was as if he had aged fifty years. His hair was 100 percent gray and his skin wrinkled. Gone was the confidence and the bravado. He was a shell of a man. I no longer feared him; I pitied him. For all his scheming and gamesmanship, he had lost his soul and he did not even know it. His need to win and be right cost him everything. He had become a man caught up inside himself, taking from everyone. He had forgotten to look around and see the simple joy of living.

When the session was over, the truth had carried the day as I knew it would. All support that I was to receive was court mandated, therefore it drawn from the state and given to me. The truth had won out, and there was no more fighting. On this day I began to hope for a family that could get along. Before this it was like my ex, God, and I were sitting in three different rooms trying to communicate to each other, but no one was listening.

I thought back to when my ex wallowed downstairs in the family room, drinking while he lived with us until he moved to his own house. While he was with us, he seemed try to hide the darkness. I am sure when he moved, he did the same thing. He made a retreat by closing the blinds and allowing no one in. He was alone with his demons, falling asleep alone. I wonder if he prayed. I know God would have come if he would have asked for a sign. God does not let man face life standing on his own. But did my ex ever pray and lay down the bottle from his darkened room? Did he face the devil straight on and pray?

While my ex was in his dark room, I was sitting in my bedroom praying. I was praying the rosary, I was praying the beatitudes, I was praying the Lord's Prayer, I was just talking to God—I never stopped praying.

I sat there and prayed while I stared at a picture of Jesus on the bedroom wall. It was small, but for me it was powerful. It centered me. I waited for the answer to my prayers. I knew God could heal my ex, and I knew if I kept my faith, we could have everything that I prayed for. But I was so unclear. I felt like time and time again God was telling me to be patient. But in reality, our love slipped away and there was nothing I could do.

And God, where was he? He was in some grand ballroom watching this dance of sorrow between us occur. Like he was waiting for us to show our love to him somehow. But I could not figure out the coded message to pull everyone together.

So that masklike image, what was it? Was it my imagination? I do not think so. I really think it was the devil. Call me silly. But what else could it have been? For years my ex relied on the showmanship of lies. Why wouldn't the devil live inside him? Many true believers of Christ have God living in them. Why wouldn't the reverse be true?

The devil was caught when I saw that split-second glimpse of that black image. Like any liar, he left. After that court date no one heard from my ex again. Not my children, the church, or the school. He was just gone. My daughter received no emails. I had no problems, and there was no contact with my ex at all.

Two months later, we got a call saying that he had slipped and hit his head while he was drinking at home. He had bled out and died. No one had checked on him, and his bloated body was found four days later with his cat.

God had given him every opportunity to change, he turned away each time. God let him make his own choice. God was done.

Harsh to say—how do I know what is in God's mind?

The funeral was bleak. His brothers were there, as well as my parents and his. Of course, our son and daughter were there, but I had to beg them to go. They did not want to take time off school. I think the whole concept made them uncomfortable, and they wanted to escape the pain. However, I did not let them.

As I sat there next to my parents, I was numb. This was it. The end of decades of fighting. What was solved? Why did God put me through it? Did God put me through it? And as if on cue, this song started to play.

Here I Am, Lord
by Dan Schutte b. 1947

I, the Lord of sea and sky,
I have heard My people cry.
All who dwell in dark and sin
My hand will save.

Sarah Erstwhile

I who made the stars of night,
I will make their darkness bright.
Who will bear My light to them?
Whom shall I send?

Here I am Lord, Is it I Lord?
I have heard You calling in the night.
I will go Lord, if You lead me.
I will hold Your people in my heart.

I, the Lord of snow and rain,
I have born my people's pain.
I have wept for love of them,
They turn away.

I will break their hearts of stone,
Give them hearts for love alone.
I will speak My word to them,
Whom shall I send?

Here I am Lord, Is it I Lord?
I have heard You calling in the night.
I will go Lord, if You lead me.
I will hold Your people in my heart.

I, the Lord of wind and flame,
I will tend the poor and lame.
I will set a feast for them,
My hand will save

Finest bread I will provide,
Till their hearts be satisfied.
I will give My life to them,
Whom shall I send?

Here I am Lord, Is it I Lord?
I have heard You calling in the night.
I will go Lord, if You lead me.
I will hold Your people in my heart.

Yes, I was sent. I remember. Yes, I tried my best to use my gift of endurance. Yes, God, but I do not know why. At the end of the day, he still died. I do not know who the lesson was for. My children's father still died.

CHAPTER 30

Where Are We Now?

To some people, learning how to forgive someone is one thing and to forget is another thing. But the truth is that when you actually forgive, and you remember the incidence later, it will be with no pain or hurt attached.[47]

—Ngozi Nwoke

We must remember that it's up to the fallen to work on change. It is not just the responsibility of those around the fallen to blaze the trail to redemption. Yes, we all can do more to help the wayward than be thankful they recognize their problems. But at the end of the day, it is their rabbit hole to climb out of and their lessons to learn. Many Bible passages guide us to keep away from people who cause divisions and put obstacles between us and God (Rom 16:17 NIV).[48] Our goal should be to help but not lose our way, and if we find that we are, we are to walk away, back to the Lord. God will try something else.

I look back at the journey I endured for my children. I could not walk away and leave them to deal with their father alone. I did not want them to feel abandoned and worthless. Even though that is what the courts were telling me to do, I could not just let me kids go sit for a week at a time at a place where they were being used as pawns by a drunk playing a game of child-support chess.

God knew that about me, of course. He gave me all sorts of temporary contract jobs to keep me going. By the time my ex had passed away, I had a wonderful resume of high-powered consulting jobs. Did I know that was God's plan? Of course not. I was flying by the seat of my pants, taking whatever came to me and working as fast as I could to find the next gig.

I cleaned houses for cash, and I hid that away for emergencies. I was stressed and mad about being in the middle of the mess.

When the funeral was over, I expected to be magically transported to the land of the normal. In this land, there were only smiles and love. But the train for that land never came. I kept searching for a teaching job and expecting God to deliver. I forgot the lessons I learned—I was missing a piece. God was waiting for me to gather the right prefixes to my coursework. It's an academic thing. I went back to school online—Harvard this time. Once I finished, I began receiving offers, and I am now teaching at a wonderful university.

God just needed me to listen.

And what about the kids? They are chasing their dreams without any repercussion of their dad's afflictions. My prayers were answered there too.

When I look back at the drama, and I rarely do, I just shake my head. I did endure, but I have no idea why I was chosen. I guess because I *could* endure. I am sure I will find out on my final day.

Because, you know, I will ask.

And what about those stumbling blocks? How am I now?

God had opened my eyes to my blindness. I no longer believed people I loved could not be dishonest. I just did not know how to handle it. I still became angry with people who were straight-up lying. I stopped short of asking myself the tough questions of why they were lying. I was just mad that they did it. But I had learned to walk away and let God sort them out.

I had developed the ability to set boundaries. I had to. I learned that if I stated right up front what I would do and what I wouldn't do, and stuck to it, people understood me better. People like what they can understand. Before, people always expected a yes, and when they by chance they received a no, they felt entitled and got angry. Now with clear boundaries, there were no disappointments.

My self-esteem and my ego leveled out. I had healthy opinions with a normal dose of pride. I could keep my thoughts to myself or express them to others without being offensive. The self-esteem stumbling block was conquered! And so was the impatience stumbling block. My heart-to-hearts with God became musings with plenty of time lag. One might say we have running conversations!

Now for strength and anger, my two biggest stumbling blocks. I am no longer angry at myself. But the anger at my husband never left. Not even though he died. He chose alcohol and the devil over his family and God. That I have a hard time reconciling. I no longer dwell on the anger at the families for not helping. I cannot go back in time and fix it. I just look ahead and spend what little time I have left with my parents. As for the anger at the people around me from the church and school for not getting involved, I have moved away from the area. I do not see them. Once, prior to leaving, I met someone by chance at the grocery store. She made a comment that they had had such a time with my ex-husband, trying to keep everyone safe. I choked back what I wanted to say and just nodded.

And what about strength? Molding that strength into something useful to God is another story. My worldly strength was my stumbling block until God started shaping it for his glory. Now ...

Here I am.

NOTES

1   New International Version Bible. James 1:3–4 Bible Gateway Online. https://www.biblegateway.com/passage/?search=James+1%3A3-4+& version=NIV.

2   Kristin Armstrong, *Happily Ever after: Walking with Peace and Courage through a Year of Divorce* (Faith Words) 2008.

3   English Standard Version Bible.1 Corinthians 15:33–34 Bible Gateway Online. https://www.biblegateway.com/passage/?search=1+Corinthian s+15%3A33-34++&version=ESV.

4   S. Klein, & S. Lehmann, *The Science of Happiness: How Our Brains Make Us Happy - and What We Can Do to Get Happier* (Translation ed. Da Capo Lifelong Books, 2002).

5   New Living Translation Bible. Isaiah 5:20-23 Bible Gateway Online. https://www.biblegateway.com/quicksearch/?quicksearch=What+sorrow+for+those+who+say+that+evil+is+good+and+good+is+evil&version=NLT.

6   "Hoops Star Wayman Tisdale Dies At 44." *Https://Www.cbsnews.com/News/Hoops-Star-Wayman-Tisdale-Dies-at-44/#:~:Text=U.S.,PM%20/%20AP*, 2009 The Associated Press, 16 May 2009, https://www.cbsnews.com/news/hoops-star-wayman-tisdale-dies-at-44/. Accessed 31 July 2022.

7   Pete Wilson, *Plan b; What Do You Do When God Dosen't Show up the Way You Thought He Would* (New York: Grupo Nelson, 2011).

8   Quentin Crisp Quotes, "*Quotes.net*" July 31 2022, https://www.quotes.net/quote/34903.

9   English Standard Version Bible. Proverbs 16:32 Bible Gateway Online.

10 God's Word Translation Bible. Ephesians 4:29 Bible Gateway Online.

11 English Standard Version Bible. Galatians 6:7–8 Bible Gateway Online.

12 English Standard Version Bible. Proverbs 16:32 Bible Gateway Online.

13 "Styles of Communication." *Angelfire*, https://www.angelfire.com/az2/webenglish/commstyles.html.

14 English Standard Version Bible. Matthew 18:15–17 Bible Gateway Online.

15 New International Version Bible. Ephesians 4:25 Bible Gateway Online

16 God's Word Translation Bible. Ephesians 4:15 Bible Gateway Online

17 Barnes, Emilie. In the Stillness of Quiet Moments: A Devotional. Harvest House Publishers, 2012.

18 English Standard Version Bible. Matthew 18:15–17 Bible Gateway Online

19 English Standard Version Bible. Proverbs 14:25 Bible Gateway Online.

20 Pete Wilson, Plan b; What Do You Do When God Dosen't Show up the Way You Thought He Would (New York: Grupo Nelson, 2011).

21 "Identify Abuse." The Hotline, accessed May 2, 2022, https://www.thehotline.org/identify-abuse.

22 English Standard Version Bible. Matthew 15:18-20 Bible Gateway Online.

23 English Standard Version Bible. Ephesians 5:21-33 Bible Gateway Online.

24 Pete Wilson, Plan b; What Do You Do When God Doesn't Show up the Way You Thought He Would (New York: Grupo Nelson, 2011).

25 English Standard Version Bible. Proverbs 20:1 Bible Gateway Online.

26 English Standard Version Bible. 1 Corinthians 14:33 Bible Gateway Online.

27 English Standard Version Bible. 1 Corinthians 7:15 Bible Gateway Online.

28 English Standard Version Bible. Matthew 15:21–28 Bible Gateway Online.

29 English Standard Version Bible. Romans 9:1 Bible Gateway Online.

30 Weitzman, Susan. 'Not to People like Us': Hidden Abuse in Upscale Marriages, Basic Book, 2000.

31 Rosenthal, A. M. "On My Mind; Silence Is a Lie." *New York Times*, Oct. 8 1981.

32 English Standard Version Bible. James 1:12-15 Bible Gateway Online.

33 "Selected Sermons by St. Augustine." accessed May 2, 2022 https://aquinas-in-english.neocities.org/augustinus.html.

34 "D. Anthony Storm's Commentary on Kierkegaard." Kierkegaard, D. Anthony Storm's Commentary on - The Sickness Unto Death, accessed May 2, 2022 http://sorenkierkegaard.org/sickness-unto-death.html.

35 The American Heritage Dictionary of the English Language: Fourth Edition. Houghton Mifflin, Co., 2000.

36 English Standard Version Bible. Ecclesiastes 7; 16–17 Bible Gateway Online.

37 New Living Translation Bible. 2 Peter 1:10 Bible Gateway Online

38 The Message Bible. Psalm 140:1–13 Bible Gateway Online

39 New International Version Bible. 2 Peter 3:8–9 Bible Gateway Online

40 New International Version Bible. 1 Peter 4:10–11 Bible Gateway Online

41 Lucado, Max. A Love Worth Giving. Thomas Nelson, Inc, 2002.

42   Pete Wilson, Plan b; What Do You Do When God Doesn't Show up the Way You Thought He Would (New York: Grupo Nelson, 2011).

43   "Mary McLeod Bethune Quotations at Quotetab." QuoteTab, accessed May 15, 2022, https://www.quotetab.com/quotes/by-mary-mcleod-bethune.

44   Pete Wilson, Plan b; What Do You Do When God Doesn't Show up the Way You Thought He Would (New York: Grupo Nelson, 2011).

45   English Standard Version Bible. Proverbs 5: 21–23 Bible Gateway Online.

46   English Standard Version Bible. Proverbs 6:12–15 Bible Gateway Online.

47   "Spiritual and/or Moral Articles." The Seven Simple Ways To Forgiving, Spiritual and/or Moral Articles, Malankara World, accessed May 15, 2022, http://www.malankaraworld.com/library/Spiritual/Spiritual_7-simple-ways-to-forgive.htm.

48   New International Version Bible. Romans 16:17 Bible Gateway Online

Printed in the United States
by Baker & Taylor Publisher Services